THE STRUGGLE WITHIN

THE STRUGGLE WITHIN

A MEMOIR OF THE EMERGENCY

ASHOK CHAKRAVARTI

HarperCollins *Publishers* India

First published in India in 2021 by
HarperCollins *Publishers*
A-75, Sector 57, Noida, Uttar Pradesh 201301, India
www.harpercollins.co.in

2 4 6 8 10 9 7 5 3 1

Copyright © Ashok Chakravarti 2021

P-ISBN: 978-93-5422-747-9
E-ISBN: 978-93-5422-502-4

The views and opinions expressed in this book are the author's own. The facts are as reported by him and the publishers are not in any way liable for the same.

Although the book is based on real events and people, the names of certain characters and organizations have been changed to protect their privacy and identity. Some of the events in the narrative have also been creatively dramatized without distorting the non-fictional character of the story.

Ashok Chakravarti asserts the moral right
to be identified as the author of this work.

Typeset in 11/15.2 Berling LT Std at
Manipal Technologies Limited, Manipal

Printed and bound at
Thomson Press (India) Ltd.

This book is produced from independently certified FSC™ paper
to ensure responsible forest management.

To the memory of those who fought for the restoration of democratic rights in India and against the Emergency of 1975. Their struggle gives credence to the famous saying 'Eternal vigilance is the price of liberty'.

Contents

	Preface	ix
1	Leaflets, Gheraos and Strikes	1
2	The Party	19
3	Rachel	29
4	Delhi Bandh	39
5	The Bhangi of Seelampur	51
6	26 June 1975	67
7	Kites, Custard Apples and Mantras	80
8	Of Mountains and Men	97
9	Ram Sewak	114
10	Jyoti	127
11	The Emergency	139

12	Turkman Gate	156
13	Doubts and Resurrection	170
14	The Struggle Within	186
15	End of the Emergency	197
	Epilogue	207
	Notes	211
	Index	213
	About the Author	221

Preface

THE DECADE OF 1967 to 1977 was one of the most turbulent in the history of post-Independence India. During this period, the future of India's democracy was on a knife-edge. Prior to the 1970s, the resilience of the political institutions established under the Constitution had never been tested. In all the elections held since Independence, the Congress Party had won comfortable majorities. Then, in 1969, the Congress Party split and Indira Gandhi was expelled from its ranks. Not to be deterred, Mrs Gandhi declared 'Garibi Hatao' (Eliminate Poverty) as her splinter group's slogan, and won a landslide victory in the March 1971 elections. However, this was a pyrrhic win. The economy had been performing poorly for over a decade, and the situation was dire. Inflation was skyrocketing. Poverty and unemployment were rife, and the country was in a state of turmoil. Strikes, demonstrations and agrarian unrest were the order of the day. Inspired by the peasant revolt in Naxalbari in 1967, the landless and poor in West Bengal, Bihar and other states had begun attacking landlords and taking over their estates. In the urban areas, there were regular protests by students and workers, resulting in violence and police firings. In 1973, the Provincial Armed Constabulary of Uttar Pradesh revolted and the army had to be called to suppress this mutiny.

It was in this environment that in early 1973, a group of idealistic left-wing political activists based in Delhi decided to form a group. Their objective was to participate in the ongoing struggles of workers and peasants in the country, and eventually bring about revolutionary change in India. Initially, they mobilized and participated in the workers' movement in and around the capital city. This included strikes by textile workers; by the Harijan sweepers and cleaners or safai karamcharis of the municipal corporation, as they were called; and the all-India railway strike of 1974. The latter almost brought the whole country to a standstill. However, the state of Emergency declared on 26 June 1975, and the suspension of democratic rights guaranteed under the Constitution, deflected them from their purpose. The goal of a socialist revolution was set aside for the time being, and they redirected their energies towards the more immediate task of the restoration of democratic rights in the country. This book is an account of their struggle against the regime of Mrs Indira Gandhi, who tried to impose a dictatorship on the people of India. The story is told through the eyes of Arjun, one of the political activists. Arjun was my incognito name while I was part of the underground movement during this period.

The Emergency lasted from June 1975 to March 1977. It was post-Independence India's darkest hour. Over 150,000 people were arrested and kept in prison, without trial, for almost two years. The number of people killed in police firings or eliminated in prisons is unknown, but could well run into the thousands.

Eleven million men and women were subjected to forcible family planning, including vasectomies, tubectomies and other forms of sterilization.

The heroes of the Emergency were many – mostly unknown – who were beaten, tortured or killed in fake encounters, in prison cells, or elsewhere, fighting against the dictatorship. A few of them are part of this story. The villains and their henchmen are well known. Mrs Gandhi, her son Sanjay Gandhi, and their coterie, who were the forces behind the Emergency, were eventually defeated in the elections of March 1977 by a united front of the people of India led by Jayaprakash Narayan and a broad coalition of opposition political parties.

The reader may note that certain expressions which are not politically correct, in particular, words referring to caste categories such as 'bhangi' and 'chamar', are used in the text. This also includes phrases such as 'disabled' or 'mentally retarded', which were in common social usage during the 1960s and 1970s. I would like to categorically state that such words and phrases are not being used to hurt the sensibilities of any person or community. The caste words are being used in the original sense, as part of a social language used to identify a community during the period covered by this book. They are purely descriptive in nature. There is no derisory, denigrating or insulting content, or intention, whatsoever. On the contrary, these words are being used with the great respect and empathy that I have for these communities. During the Emergency, I lived and worked in the bhangi bastis of Delhi; they were my friends and comrades, and I was extremely proud that this community accepted me as one of their own.

I would like to acknowledge the support, the ideas and the incisive critiques I received from Shobna Chakravarti, Sundeep

Dougal, Hansa Patel and Tarini Chakravarti. Their contributions were invaluable for the writing of this book. Last but not least, I am most grateful to my editors, in particular Krishan Chopra and Rinita Banerjee, for their patience in assisting me to finalize the manuscript.

New Delhi
May 2021

1

Leaflets, Gheraos and Strikes

It was a scorching May afternoon in 1973 when Arjun arrived back in Delhi on a flight from London. The six years he had spent at Oxford University had gone like a flash. His main concern at the moment was the 1,000 pounds sterling he was carrying on him to contribute to the revolutionary movement in India. He was worried that a customs official would discover this booty and confiscate it. Then how would he start his revolutionary activities? As it happened, he had nothing to fear. The currency notes were well hidden in the sleeve of a long-playing record, and there being no X-ray machines in those days, the customs officials let him pass after a perfunctory search. Outside the customs area, his parents were waiting to pick him up. Arjun's father was the governor of Himachal Pradesh at that time, based in Simla. During the governor's visits to Delhi, it was customary for him to stay at Rashtrapati Bhavan, the residence of the President of India. Arjun was therefore bundled into the car and escorted to Rashtrapati Bhavan. Riding in the official car emblazoned with the three-headed lion emblem of the Indian state, Arjun could not but think of the irony of his situation. He had just returned to India with his head full of all kinds of revolutionary ideas, but his first act was to spend a couple of days at the residence of the President of India, a primary symbol of the state that he sought to overthrow.

After a few days, Arjun's parents took him over to his brother's house at the University of Delhi. No one questioned why, after all these years at Oxford, he had returned without any precise sense of what he was proposing to do in the future. Nor was he asked why he had not completed his PhD, which at most would have taken another year of study. Most of Arjun's peers had by now obtained employment in large multinational firms, banks in the City of London, or international organizations such as the World Bank. Unfortunately for Arjun, both his mother and his father were too involved in their own lives. There was no advice or direction from them. Their son would have to figure things out for himself, and find his own way through life.

Arjun's brother was a mild-mannered academic. He and his wife were both professors at the university. Their lives were focused on teaching their students and their research. However, they were also intensely committed to the idea of an open, democratic society in India: a society in which there was a free flow of ideas and open debate, and where the concerns of the poor would be given primacy. India under Indira Gandhi fell short of this mark by a long way. Soon after Arjun's return, his brother expressed mild curiosity as to what his plans were and what he was proposing to do. When Arjun explained to them his newly found social consciousness and his desire to participate in the ongoing political movements to bring about radical change in the country, they were somewhat surprised. Arjun had never struck them as a person who would give up a promising international career to become a political activist.

After all, he had been at Oxford for six years, spent some time teaching there, and had even done a stint with the World Bank in Washington, DC. In spite of their scepticism, however, they agreed to help him in any way that he needed.

Arjun wanted to start a weekly magazine for the working classes in Delhi. He believed that the existing left-wing press did not analyse the economic and political developments in the country in a manner that increased the class consciousness of the poor and enhanced their militancy or desire to escalate the class struggle. Besides, there was nothing in print out there that specifically focused on Delhi and issues of local relevance. Through his brother, Arjun got introduced to a few university teachers who were known to be active in left-wing circles. Most of them were already allied to one or other of the existing socialist or communist parties. So while they heard out what Arjun had to say, they did not show much enthusiasm for the idea. However, there were a few college lecturers who were either independent minded, or members of the legal Communist Party of India (Marxist) (CPI [M]), but secretly sympathetic to the new extreme left-wing groups that had emerged after the Naxalbari uprising of 1967. They expressed interest in the project and encouraged Arjun to pursue it further. Amongst them was Harsh, an economics lecturer at Hindu College, and Islam, a sociology lecturer at Zakir Husain College. Arjun was to become fast friends with both Harsh and Islam. While Hindu College was in the main university campus, Zakir Husain College was located at Ajmeri Gate, in the old walled city of Delhi, where a large part of the city's Muslim population lived. This association with Islam was to become of great significance during the Emergency.

After several days of lobbying, Arjun managed to persuade many of those he had spoken with to attend a meeting to discuss the newspaper project. Harsh had agreed to allow his apartment to be used for the gathering. Soon the room was full. Arjun was asked to explain what he had in mind and why any of them should support it. He made an impassioned plea for renewed action, stating that the Indian economy was in a dire situation, and class conflict was escalating in both rural and urban areas. In Bihar alone, 600 agrarian agitations had been recorded in 1970. The need of the hour was, therefore, new thinking and new initiatives. Shastri, one of the older lecturers to attend, was the first to respond. Shastri had been a supporter of the pro-Russian Communist Party of India (CPI) for a long time.

He said, 'Listen, Arjun, it is good to see a young and enthusiastic person like you coming forward to support the people's cause. But our movement is not new: it has been going on for over fifty years. The CPI was founded in 1925. We have well-organized party structures, workers' unions and channels for publicity. You could contribute a lot by joining us. On your own you will not get very far.'

Ramesh, another lecturer, who now supported the breakaway CPI (M), spoke up. 'Yes, fifty years old and getting geriatric! From being founders of the workers' and peasants' movement, you have now become an appendage of Indira Gandhi's Congress government. Can you not see that there are strikes and industrial action all over the country? We need to provide leadership to all these struggles, not support a fascist regime that is suppressing the people.'

Shastri was angered by this jibe about the CPI. He left along with a colleague. Arjun, fearing that the meeting would now be disrupted and other people would leave, quickly stepped in. He said, 'I know I am new here and naïve. I do not have the political experience and party associations you have, but I believe I have something to contribute. I may end up joining one of your groups, but for now I just want to start a weekly magazine. I have enough resources to run it for about six months, and all I need is your cooperation to write articles and analytical pieces on subjects I will propose to you as the editor. In writing your article you do not have to deviate from your party, group or personal position. So I will just be providing an additional platform for your views.'

Harsh then chimed in, saying, 'Come on, guys. Arjun seems like a dedicated sort. Let's give it a try. After all, it is true there is no left-wing paper specifically addressing events and issues pertaining to the Delhi region.'

The others agreed. It was decided the new paper would be called *Janvaad* or 'People's Democracy', and it would come out as a monthly, not a weekly – at least to start with. The group would do the writing, but Arjun as editor would have to organize the registration of the paper, its financing, printing and distribution. Arjun was overjoyed at this result. Within a month of his return to India, his project of starting a newspaper was going to become a reality. He had already converted his 1,000 pounds into rupees at a very favourable black-market rate, and with the magazine coming out once a month, he had more than enough funds to bring out issues for a whole year. To him, his participation in the revolution had begun!

Some months after the magazine had started, Harsh, Islam and Arjun were chatting in the university coffee house and ogling the pretty girls who frequented this popular hangout. Harsh said, 'You know, after you approached us the first time about starting the magazine, my friends and I thought that you were either extremely arrogant, or extremely stupid, or in fact both, to come back to India and jump into active politics in this manner.'

'Then why did you agree to work with me?' said Arjun.

'Well, we decided you would either fizzle out or disappear as fast as you had appeared. But the idea was a good one, so it was certainly worth a try. Don't forget that we have only just started, haven't we? We still have a very long way to go.'

THE FIRST FEW ISSUES of *Janvaad* were popular. Circulation in the university was not a problem. But its whole purpose was to influence the working classes, and this meant that direct access to workers in various factories would have to be established. The existing trade unions were hostile to this new initiative because they saw it as competing with and dismissive of their own agendas. The nearest major industrial unit to the university was Birla textile mills. It was owned by one of the largest business conglomerates in the country, the Birla Group. Its owners were very close to the Indian National Congress, the party in power. The mill had 9,000 workers. Through Harsh and his CPI (M) friends, Arjun was introduced to a small group of workers in this textile mill who were influenced by Marxist thinking.

The workers' group mainly consisted of landless labourers from eastern Uttar Pradesh, called purabias – from the word purab, meaning 'east' – who had migrated to Delhi in search of work. The most enthusiastic of the lot were three purabias called Mohun, Tulsi and Raju. They lived in a jhuggi-jhompri colony near the mill in which most of the huts were made from clay bricks and mud, with corrugated tin roofs. They had left their families back home in the villages of eastern UP. Although welcoming, the three purabias treated Arjun with some scepticism during their initial meetings. Arjun, sensing this, asked them what their reservations about him were. The workers indicated that a few years ago, some other young fellows like him from the local colleges nearby had accosted them in a similar manner. The students were very enthusiastic and seemed committed to their cause. But they tended to appear and disappear as they pleased, and then the day came when they were never seen again. So they wondered if Arjun would behave in a similar manner.

Many years later Arjun discovered that the students referred to were the initial group of leftists from St Stephen's College, an elite Delhi University institution and his own alma mater, who had been inspired by the uprising in Naxalbari and had made attempts to foment revolution amongst the working classes in Delhi. They had obviously not been successful in this endeavour, but they had certainly left behind a great deal of scepticism about the true intentions of so-called young 'revolutionaries' like him amongst the workers in Birla Mills. To prove himself, Arjun redoubled his efforts to spend time with the purabias, eating and sleeping in their jhuggis, sometimes for days on end. Every evening would be spent with the group, explaining the exploitation of the working classes, the need for a revolution to establish a socialist state, and how poverty had been eliminated in communist China. Heated discussions were held about the true nature of Mrs Gandhi's government, the worsening economic situation, the increasing unrest across the country, and the repressive measures that the government was taking to crush the people's struggle. The purabias liked Arjun, and soon the group expanded from the original small number to over twenty workers from the same mill. Arjun organized them into cells, which could distribute the magazine in the different departments of the mill. A small workers' committee to coordinate activities was formed. Arjun was now ready to take the next step of establishing a more public platform to express his views and those contained in the magazine.

Inspired by the Speakers' Corner in Hyde Park, London, Arjun organized his own wooden crate and set this up just outside the front gate of Birla Mills. Behind the crate he put up a large blackboard to regularly post news about the ongoing workers' and peasants' agitations in the country, their demands and the government's reaction. Every Monday and Friday he would arrive at the mill gate at lunchtime, climb onto his crate and harangue the workers for an hour or so with political speeches, the need for greater militancy to improve their pay and working conditions, and the uselessness of the established trade unions. While his workers' group made sure there were at least twenty or thirty people in the audience, interest in his speeches would sometimes result in gatherings of more than 100 workers at a time. In particular, what his audiences liked was the freedom to throw questions at him about current political issues and to discuss these openly and freely. These were not monologues delivered by some political leader; they were conversations in which all could participate.

Arjun would start his speeches by shouting out a few political slogans to get the attention of the workers, most of whom would be loitering around drinking tea or smoking bidis during their lunch break.

'*Indira Gandhi murdabad!*' (Down with Indira Gandhi!)
'*Mazdoor ekta zindabad!*' (Long live workers' unity!)
'*Inquilab zindabad!*' (Long live the revolution!)
'*Tata, Birla murdabad!*' (Down with Tata and Birla!)

The ice was now broken and Arjun would commence speaking. Occasionally he would be interrupted by contrary voices.

'Arre, chote sahib! Who do you think you are, coming here to give us all these grand ideas? The Hindu religion tells us that we are ruled by our karma and nothing will change.' To which

Arjun would respond with vigour, asserting that people had the power to change their destinies. They had done so in Russia and China, and could do so in India as well.

At other times, someone would say, 'Indira Gandhi is a good lady. See, she has taken away the properties of the old rajas and landlords, and will distribute all this to the poor.' To this Arjun would retort that Indira Gandhi was just another representative of the capitalist class. She was simply cheating the workers with populist slogans and they would never benefit from her government.

And so the harangues would continue about the need for unity between the workers and the peasants, the need for militant and continued struggles against the capitalists and the government, and how a people's revolution would occur very soon.

ARJUN BECAME INCREASINGLY POPULAR with the workers at Birla Mills. The established trade unions resented his presence and would have been quite happy to send out a group of goondas (thugs) to beat him up. But they were scared of him. It was not only that he had the support of the workers in the mill, but from the language in his speeches and the material posted on his blackboard it was evident that he was sympathetic to the political positions and strategies being advocated by the extreme leftists. To them he was a dangerous and violent extremist who could well be in contact with the Naxalite killer squads in the rural areas. It was best, therefore, to steer clear of him.

Arjun's popularity at Birla Mills soon got him an invitation to meet up with another group of workers from the Swadeshi Textile Mills, which operated in the heart of Old Delhi. This textile mill was part of a huge industrial conglomerate owned by a prominent business family. It had 6,000 workers. The conditions of work in the Swadeshi factory were much worse than those in Birla Mills. Pay was much lower, there were a significant number of temporary employees who could be sacked at any time, and worst of all, the management had a group of goondas ready to break up any protest action by the workers and beat up anyone who dared to complain. One of the managers who controlled the operations in the factory was the biggest offender. Any worker who was summoned to his office knew he was about to be summarily dismissed or given a good thrashing. The man was also known to have molested many women workers in his office. The established trade unions were in cahoots with the management and so did little to address the grievances of the workers.

Many of the workers in the Swadeshi Mills were also purabias, from eastern UP. Mohun, Tulsi and Raju therefore found it very easy to organize a network of potential supporters in the various departments of the factory. Arjun, who was already known for his speeches at Birla Mills, was then brought in to meet representatives of the new group, discuss their problems, and consider what needed to be done to address their oppression. After several meetings it was agreed that the situation was intolerable and strong action needed to be taken against the management and owners of the mill. Arjun proposed a plan for the occupation of the factory by the workers, and a people's trial of the notorious manager and his thugs. The action would take place on the following Saturday at 4 p.m., when the shift change occurred.

It was a steamy August afternoon with temperatures over 40°C when Arjun and his small group of militants from Birla Mills hid in the jhuggi-jhompri colony just across the road from the Swadeshi factory gate. At fifteen minutes to the hour the factory siren rang, signifying the end of the previous shift and the beginning of the new one. The high gates, which protected the premises, were opened by the guards to let in the new shift workers. At that moment Arjun and his group, armed with lathis, rushed across the road and quickly overpowered the guards at the gate. They then let in the incoming workers and closed the gates. Shouts of *'Tata-Birla hai hai!'*, *'Chartu–Bhartu hai hai!'* (Down with Tata and Birla!, Down with Charatram and Bharatram!), and *'Indira Gandhi murdabad!'* (Down with Indira Gandhi!) rang out in the air. With the advantage of surprise, the support group within the factory captured the manager's thugs as well and tied them up, hands and feet. More slogans were now being shouted.

'Hamari maangen poori karo!' (Our demands must be met!)
'Tanashahi nahi chalegi!' (Dictatorship will not succeed!)

Within a few minutes the entire factory was under the control of the workers. The anger in the factory now boiled over and a huge mob attacked the manager's office. He was dragged out and the workers started hitting him with slippers and sticks. Bleeding and with his clothes torn, the manager pleaded for mercy. Arjun went up to him and told him that the only thing that could save him now was if he called his head office and informed them that he was under a gherao, that the factory was fully occupied by the workers, and that the senior management of Swadeshi should immediately come and negotiate with the workers about their demands. Further, if the management permitted the police to attack the premises, the workers were ready to resist. There would be widespread violence and the factory itself could be set on fire. The manager made the phone call to his head office. Outside the factory gates, tension grew. A posse of fifty policemen armed with lathis and rifles had now gathered, awaiting orders from their superiors. One of the purabias from Birla Mills went to the top of the gate, and using a megaphone, shouted down at the police.

'We are fighting for the genuine rights of the workers,' he said. 'You must not attack us. You police are also workers and you are our brothers. The management is coming to negotiate with us. We want peace, but if you attack us, remember there are 2,000 workers inside this factory, and we will resist you with the last drop of our blood!'

After hearing this, the police were not quite sure what to do. The huge factory gates barred their entry into the interior of the premises, and they did not have any equipment to break it down. The idea of confronting 2,000 militant workers also deterred any action. The inspector in charge of the posse decided it was best to call for reinforcements and wait for orders to come from the higher-ups. Soon the managing director of the Swadeshi company arrived at the scene. Through the megaphone he was told that he would be allowed to enter the premises with his officers. No harm would come to them, but they must order the police to stay out of the factory and not attack the gates. This was agreed and the managing director entered the factory. Deafening slogans were shouted by the workers. The workers' committee took the company officials to the manager's office and placed their four basic demands before them:

- The manager controlling operations and his thugs should all be dismissed and removed from the factory immediately.
- All casual workers who had been working regularly for the past twelve months should be given permanent employment.

- Wage levels should be reviewed to bring them in line with the other textile factories in Delhi.
- The police should be withdrawn and no retaliatory action should be taken against any worker who had participated in this strike.

Arjun then accosted the managing director and told him that the old days had gone. Workers' militancy was occurring all over the country, and if Swadeshi did not agree to these simple demands, the consequences could be dire. The factory could remain under forced occupation of the workers, there could be battles with the police and loss of life, and finally, the factory itself and its equipment could be seriously damaged by angry workers. Seeing the gravity of the situation and the anger amongst the workers, the managing director capitulated and accepted all the workers' demands. There was jubilation amongst the workers at their victory, and the mood in the factory immediately changed. New slogans were now shouted.

'*Swadeshi Mills zindabad!*' (Long live Swadeshi Mills!)
'*Tata–Birla zindabad!*'
'*Charatram–Bharatram zindabad!*'
'*Indira Gandhi zindabad!*'
'*Arjun bhaiyya zindabad!*'

Arjun was dismayed at these new slogans showering praise on the capitalist class in the country and the Prime Minister of India. But in this moment of the workers' triumph and his own popularity, he thought it best to keep his mouth shut and his concerns to himself. The manager and his thugs were summarily evicted, the police left, and a new manager was left behind by the managing director to normalize the operations of the factory and work on the implementation of the workers' demands. The strike was over.

AFTER THE SWADESHI STRIKE, Arjun became a political leader in his own right and a well-known activist amongst working-class circles in northern Delhi. His popularity soon got him an invitation to meet and interact with the local leaders of the Bhangis. Most of the Bhangis worked as cleaners and sweepers for the Delhi municipality. These workers were the lowest of the low, the outcasts of the Indian caste system, who cleaned the public toilets, the sewage, the shit and filth off the streets of Delhi. They were now euphemistically called Harijans or people of God, who by virtue of being considered untouchable by the rest of Hindu society were forced to live together in neighbourhoods where no other Hindus lived or liked to venture.

In this part of the city, there were several slum areas where they lived. The largest of these slums, with almost 10,000 inhabitants, was located near the university campus, at a place that was called, somewhat inappropriately, Majnu-ka-Tila – Lover's Hill.

Arjun visited Majnu-ka-Tila on a chilly November evening. A group of about ten senior members of the community greeted him and took him into a small courtyard. Knowing he was from a higher caste, probably a Brahmin, who might not eat or drink with Harijans, he was hesitantly asked if he would like a glass of water. Arjun immediately indicated he would not only like some tea, but would be happy to join them for a meal, if indeed they had cooked any food for him. This broke the ice instantly; he was invited to stay for dinner, and the conversation now began to flow. The Harijan elders told him they were a forgotten community. Since Independence, twenty-five years ago, they had continued to live in slums all over Delhi, one tap with running water for 100 households, little or no drainage, raw sewage flowing everywhere, continued job discrimination in the municipality, and worst of all, no proper equipment to assist them in their cleaning jobs. This lack of equipment resulted in their having to demean themselves every day, carrying shit and filth in small pans on their heads. They had a trade union that was supposed to fight for their rights, but it was controlled by the ruling Congress Party and did very little for them. Arjun was also told that that there were more than 100,000 Harijans working as safai karamcharis for the municipality and private companies in Delhi, and they all lived in similar slums dotted around the city.

Arjun was horrified that the socioeconomic condition of this community had remained the same so many years after Independence. They were even worse off than the factory workers he had been mobilizing for the past few months, and desperately needed his support. Thinking more strategically, he also realized that by working with such a close-knit community, he could develop a strong base for any future people's movement. He decided to spend time with this community, eating, living with them and mobilizing them into a powerful political entity. For the next few months, the safai karamcharis were the focus of his activities. Starting in Majnu-ka-Tila, he set up Marxist study groups of younger Harijans in several of the colonies that they inhabited. Much of his time was now spent in Seelampur, across the Yamuna river, the largest colony of such municipal workers in Delhi. Here, in one of the study groups, he came across Ram Sewak, a young militant who had run away from Ballia in eastern UP and settled in Seelampur.

Ram Sewak and Arjun hit it off immediately. Ram Sewak had already been exposed to left-wing ideology in Ballia and had been yearning to find someone with whom he could discuss his views on the political situation and collaborate in mobilizing his community. He told Arjun he should treat his hut as his own home, eat with the family, and sleep there whenever he needed to. Ram Sewak's wife, Angoori, was not entirely comfortable with this invitation. But following her husband's wishes she placed a string charpai in one corner of the hut, so that Arjun had his own little sleeping area whenever he decided to stay overnight. Soon Ram Sewak's hut was like a second home to him.

Over the next few months Arjun and Ram Sewak became like brothers. Ram Sewak was a quick learner, and soon, from being a member of a study group, developed into an active political leader, organizing such groups in different parts of Delhi and leading their discussions along with Arjun. Their ideas of social equality and a people's revolution excited the younger generation of Harijans, who by now were fed up with the old politicians who had done nothing for them. A network of such bright young people was soon established across all the major safai-karamchari slums in Delhi. To formalize their existence, they established a committee and called themselves the Krantikari Harijan Sangh, or Revolutionary Harijan Association. They were now ready for action.

The safai karamcharis had never made any demands or taken any strike action against their main employer, the municipality of Delhi. To advance their political consciousness and mobilize the entire community, therefore, the Krantikari Sangh decided to pick an emotive agenda for their first confrontation with the authorities. The issue they chose was that of cleaning equipment. A formal letter was addressed to the municipality and distributed widely to all the slums in Delhi, stating that the safai karamcharis were no longer willing to carry dirt and filth in little pans on their heads. Rather, each cleaning worker should be given a small wheelbarrow and scoops for collecting rubbish. The petition was delivered to the mayor of Delhi by the workers' committee. The petition also indicated that if the municipality did not agree to this demand, all safai karamcharis in Delhi would go on strike and allow rubbish to pile up in the city. This ultimatum caused an uproar in the municipality. Some of the more conservative councillors expressed outrage saying, 'How dare these achoots (untouchables) make demands on us? We have given them employment and food for their families, and now they slap us in the face in this manner!' Others, claiming to be more sympathetic to ideas of social justice, argued that this was part of the emancipation of the lower castes, and so was a legitimate demand.

The Congress councillors, however, were cautious in their response. The Harijans had always supported them in the elections, and while they were dismayed by these demands and this new aggressive behaviour, they could not afford to alienate such a big vote bank. They persuaded the mayor to announce his agreement to the proposal, but to indicate that due to financial constraints it could only be implemented over the next twelve months. This way they could show that they were sympathetic to the workers' cause, but delay any real change for some time. Arjun and Ram Sewak were for the rejection of this response and for immediate strike action. However, the majority of the safai karamcharis, including many of the youngsters, saw it differently. They were thrilled by this outcome. This was the first time since Independence twenty-five years ago that they had made any demands, and the authorities had bowed down before them. Seeing this, Arjun and Ram Sewak withdrew their opposition. After all, this event had made a significant contribution to the political mobilization of the Harijan community, and it would encourage them to carry their economic struggle to a higher level in the future. The action had also strengthened Arjun and Ram Sewak's political base in the slum areas around Delhi. They now had a committed group of supporters and a network of safe houses where they could hide in case of any repressive action by the state.

2

The Party

RACHEL, A GERMAN JOURNALIST working as the correspondent of a European newspaper, had been living in Delhi for a year. During the late 1960s, while studying at the Sorbonne in Paris, she had come under the influence of the socialists who opposed Charles de Gaulle. She had been friendly with radical leaders such as Tariq Ali and Daniel Cohn-Bendit, better known as Dany le Rouge. During the student movement in 1968, she had participated in the protests and fought running battles with the police on the streets of Paris. However, these protests had gradually petered out and she had quietly returned to her studies.

Rachel was of medium height, slim, with blonde hair. There was nothing particularly striking about her features, but she had a wide-eyed expression and an animated way of speaking that many men found attractive. Instinctively rebellious, she had a strong anarchistic streak in her character. She had read the works of Mikhail Bakunin, the nineteenth-century Russian revolutionary activist who founded social anarchism, and was sympathetic to his ideas. She was against the concept of authority and believed that any structure or organization that promoted authority was a threat to basic human freedom. These views had put her at loggerheads with many of her fellow radicals from the late 1960s, who in due course had become members of organized political movements.

After graduating, she had joined a newspaper group, and had then been transferred to Delhi. Rachel loved being in India. The crowds, the smells, the colours – all of which combined to attack one's senses – appealed to her sense of the exotic. The current environment of political upheaval and mass movements reminded her of her own student days, and while as a foreigner she could not participate in such activities, she nevertheless tried to get to know and befriend all the radical political activists she came across.

Jawaharlal Nehru University (JNU), with its left-wing leanings, was a favourite haunt of hers. Here, in the coffee house, there were unending debates about dictatorship and democracy, alienation and existentialism, women's liberation, and of course, the Indian political scene. To show off her extensive knowledge of Delhi, she had taken one of her German friends on a sightseeing trip to Chandni Chowk in the heart of the old city. Here they had come across a palmist offering his predictions for a mere 10 rupees. The friend could not resist this temptation, and insisted that Rachel also have her palm read. The palm reader did his usual rambling about her past, her likes and dislikes, but when it came to the future, he predicted, with great gravity in his voice, that she would soon fall in love and the person would be brown-skinned. Rachel laughed at this. After all, she was in India, and all the men around her were brown-skinned. So that was not saying much. However, the thought did remain in her mind, and she would often wonder if she were indeed destined to meet someone she would be intensely attracted to in Delhi.

One of her acquaintances was Ravi Das, an upcoming painter. Ravi had a strong sexual interest in Rachel and made no effort to hide it. He would take Rachel to all the art exhibitions in town, particularly those where his paintings were being exhibited. He would say to her, 'Rachel, you have such a beautiful body. You must let me paint you in the nude one day. It will become a famous painting, no less than one of the nudes done by the classical masters.'

Rachel would smile and brush this off. She was not quite sure whether she liked or disliked these advances. Ravi was good company and through him, she had met lots of interesting people. Being Bengali, he seemed to have a natural air of intellectualism. But somehow, with his scrawny body and scruffy look, he did not quite fit her idea of a lover boy. Also she found Ravi to be somewhat degenerate. She had spent an evening with him once, during which he had smoked a lot of charas (marijuana). He was very insistent that she smoke with him, and when she had refused, he had smoked a lot more and passed out.

After this incident, Rachel had tried to avoid Ravi, spending more time researching and writing about the ongoing worker and peasant unrest in northern India or hanging out at the university coffee-house with her left-wing friends. On one of the coffee house evenings, she ran into Shekhar, a young lecturer in political science at JNU, whom she had met a few times before. Shekhar was excited. He said, 'Hi Rachel, do you know there is a new left-wing magazine which is gaining popularity in Delhi?'

'What is it called?' she said. 'Do you have a copy? Who is behind it? How can we get more information about it?' she continued animatedly.

'I don't know much about it,' said Shekhar. 'But you must have heard of the recent successful strike at the premises of the Swadeshi Mills. The factory was temporarily occupied by the workers, the manager was gheraoed, and eventually the management agreed to most to the demands. Well, it looks as if there is a new left-wing group that was behind this action, and they are the ones bringing out this magazine. I am told they are going to have an official launch of the magazine next week at the Constitution Club. Why don't we go there together and find out?'

'Sure, I would love to,' said Rachel. 'Come and pick me up on your new Enfield motorbike. I haven't had a ride on that yet!'

IT WAS NOW EARLY 1974. Arjun had been working hard to expand the circulation of the magazine. From the initial print run of 1,000 copies, it had now reached 2,500. The networks established in various working-class slums made a huge difference to its ability to reach out to a wider audience. The popularity of the magazine, the 'speakers' box' at Birla Mills, and the successful actions at Swadeshi Mills and the municipal workers drew new attention to Arjun and his activities. Reports filed by local police departments with the Central Bureau of Intelligence (CBI) of the government indicated with concern the increased militancy amongst the poor in Delhi. While the magazine was officially registered, its content was clearly inflammatory and strongly anti-government, with regular exhortations to workers to escalate their struggle against the capitalist class, and the state that represented their interests. Agitations by workers and peasants were spreading throughout northern India, and the authorities could not allow the capital city to become infected by this dangerous trend. The CBI decided that Arjun and his activities should be investigated. For this purpose, a special operative was assigned to follow his movements and collect information.

Arjun was still living with his brother at the university. However, over the past few months he had begun to spend less and less time there, and increasingly spent nights within his network in the slums. The intelligence operative had very little to go on. So he hung around Arjun's brother's house, hoping to be able to keep track of his movements from there. Arjun noticed him the very first time he was followed. The man looked like a typical Jat policeman from the neighbouring state of Haryana – well built, clean-shaven, with a crew cut. He invariably jumped on to the same bus that Arjun took and exited where he got off. Clearly, the man's undercover techniques were not very sophisticated. Arjun found it easy to shake off his tail by taking more than one bus, starting initially with one going in the opposite direction to where he was actually headed. He found it somewhat amusing that the government now saw him as a significant enough threat to place him under surveillance.

The agitations in Delhi had also come to the attention of the extreme leftists operating in the northern Indian region. By now, the Naxalite movement had split up into various factions. There was the Charu Mazumdar group, which insisted that the only tactic to be followed to mobilize the poor was the 'annihilation' of class enemies. This group was now on a murderous spree, killing landlords, police and other government officials in the rural areas. Other factions, led by people like Kanu Sanyal, Satyanarayan Sinha and Kondapalli Seetharamaiah, while accepting that the state could only be overthrown through a violent struggle, continued to advocate mass mobilization and mass movements of the workers and peasants. It was a representative of one of the latter groups who came across to Delhi and accosted Harsh, the university lecturer who was helping Arjun write articles for the journal *Janvaad*. As it happened, this activist was Bose, the same person who had interacted with Ram Sewak during his days in Ballia and had given the latter his first exposure to Marxist ideas. Bose persuaded Harsh that operating on their own in Delhi would not be an effective strategy for defeating the government, and it was necessary to join forces with like-minded groups operating in different parts of the country. He then asked Harsh to organize a meeting with Arjun to discuss this. Harsh decided to consult Islam on this idea. But it turned out that Islam was not too enthusiastic about formally joining any party. Islam indicated that he would prefer to remain a sympathizer and a supporter of the cause, but not an activist.

The meeting was set in the safai-karamchari basti of Seelampur. Harsh arrived with Bose late in the evening. Arjun was waiting with Ram Sewak in the latter's hut. As Bose entered the hut, Ram Sewak uttered a cry of recognition. 'My brother,' he said, and gave Bose a warm hug. The ice was broken. Ram Sewak had never told Arjun about his family history in Ballia and how they had come to be in Delhi. Now it all poured out. With tears in his eyes, he talked about his beloved sister Chandi, and how she had been murdered and taken from the family by the cruel landlords in Ballia. He told the others about how Bose had inspired him to mobilize his community, and of the violence that followed the killing of the landlord by a Naxalite squad.

After he had spoken, Bose said, 'The atrocities of the ruling classes on the working people have gone on for centuries. But now our time has come. Our revolution started in Naxalbari in 1967. It spread like wildfire and shook the foundations of the state. Unfortunately, the movement went off the rails with the "individual terrorism" line propagated by some comrades. But that deviation has now been corrected, and our party believes that mass mobilization and mass struggles are the only ways to further the revolution. You are all experienced and committed activists. You have made a mark in mobilizing the working people in Delhi, our capital city, and we all want you to join the party so that we can become a strong and unified organization. As a unified force, we will undoubtedly succeed in achieving our common goals.'

Ram Sewak immediately confirmed his acceptance of this idea. However, Arjun was more cautious. He said. 'Of course, we need to become part of a larger organization. But what will that mean in terms of our activities on the ground? We are not willing to be subjected to directives from leaders who are unknown to us, and who do not understand the realities in our area of operation.'

Bose responded, 'Once we are agreed on the overall strategy and tactics, we can recognize you as the Delhi Organizing Committee of the Party. You will be free to plan and pursue your own activities, within the agreed party line. But of course, you will have to take into account that you are now part of a national party and so will have to support, participate and further programmes or events that are of a national character.'

Harsh and Ram Sewak seemed to be quite satisfied by this explanation and so Arjun set aside any residual qualms he had and agreed to the proposal. With Harsh and Ram Sewak, he was now part of the Delhi State Committee of the Communist Party of India (Marxist-Leninist), or CPI (ML), as it was commonly known. Given the factionalism in the extreme left movement, Arjun was still not clear what this meant. However, so long as it did not mean that they had to do things any differently in Delhi and be subject to some outside direction, he was quite happy with this outcome.

THE OFFICIAL LAUNCH OF *Janvaad* had been set for four in the afternoon. It was to be held at the Constitution Club. The club was used by Members of Parliament (MPs) visiting Delhi, for social and residential purposes. Through their contacts in the trade union movement, the writers' group that contributed to *Janvaad* had persuaded two independent socialist MPs to be the main speakers at the gathering. Arjun and his group were concerned that members of the pro-Russian CPI, and leaders of trade unions hostile to their activities amongst the workers, would try to disrupt the proceedings. To safeguard against this, Mohun, Tulsi, Raju and a group of about fifteen workers from the Swadeshi and Birla Mills had been mobilized to attend the meeting, and sit in the rear, keeping an eye out for troublemakers.

The hall began to fill up. Arjun saw Shekhar coming in with a blonde woman. He liked the look of her and wondered who she was. Shastri, the lecturer who supported the pro-Russian communists, was also there, as well as the intelligence operative who had been following Arjun around. He was trying to sit unobtrusively at the back, but with his strong build and crew cut, he was unmistakable. The MPs arrived, and were led up to the stage. There were over 150 people in the hall now. To start the proceedings, Arjun, as the editor of the magazine, stood up and went to the microphone. He was about to welcome the guests and start the meeting when Shastri stood up from the audience and began to shout.

'We would like to know who this Arjun really is! He has come from abroad with extremist ideas and is disrupting our trade union movement. We have information that he is an agent of the American imperialist CIA. He has been sent to India to undermine the progressive government of Prime Minister Indira Gandhi.'

The group around Shastri then stood up and started shouting slogans.

'*CIA murdabad! CIA murdabad!*' (Down with the CIA!)

'*Samajwadi sarkar zindabad!*' (Long live the socialist government!)

'*Communist Party of India zindabad!*' (Long live the Communist Party of India!)

'*Naxalwadiyon ko bandh karo!*' (Lock up the Naxalites!)

'CIA, CIA, CIA, CIA!'

The people in the audience began to look dismayed and fearful. However, this was exactly the kind of disruption Arjun and his group were ready for. At a signal, the fifteen mill workers from Swadeshi and Birla Mills rushed to where Shastri and his supporters stood. They overpowered the sloganeers and physically ejected them from the hall. After this the mood inside calmed down and the function proceeded as scheduled. The socialist MPs gave stirring speeches against the government and commended the *Janvaad* team for bringing out a new journal that fought for the interests of the workers. Arjun spoke about the need to defend democracy and the rights of the people to organize, protest and struggle for the betterment of their economic conditions, and establish a more equal society. The function ended with a distribution of free copies of the journal's first edition.

After the crowds had thinned, Shekhar came up to Arjun and introduced Rachel to him.

'Hi, I am Rachel,' she said. 'Congratulations on the launch of your new journal. And that was very impressive, the way you managed the function and prevented the pro-Russian communists from disrupting the proceedings.'

Before Arjun could say anything, she continued, 'I am having a small party at my flat in Hauz Khas this Saturday. Will you please come? I would love to talk to you some more about the journal and the work you are doing. I was once part of the left-wing movement myself and involved in the protests in Paris in 1968.'

Arjun liked her direct manner and her intense blue eyes. He decided he would like to see her again. But parties were not to his liking any more. He had had his share of partying while at Oxford, and he disliked all the intrusive questioning he was normally subjected to at such events. This was particularly so now that he had joined the CPI (ML), a party that was semi-legal and had a largely underground organizational structure. He said, 'It's a pleasure meeting you, and yes, I would be happy to meet up with you again. But I do not like parties and similar social gatherings, so I am afraid I must decline that invitation.'

His refusal made Rachel even more determined to see him again. She said, 'Okay, I understand, but if you are free on Sunday afternoon, why don't you drop in for a cup of tea?' This proposal sounded much more appealing to Arjun and he accepted the invitation. Meanwhile, the intelligence operative was still writing his notes furiously in the back row. He was pleased with his work that day. He had written the names of many who had attended the function, made notes on speeches made, and had much to report to his bosses.

3

Rachel

Sunday afternoon with Rachel, Arjun thought. Almost like a date. He hadn't been alone in the company of a woman since mid 1973 when he had returned to India. After lunch, he had a shower, shaved off his weeklong stubble, put on a clean white kurta-pyjama set, and headed for Hauz Khas. He did not see the intelligence man around anywhere, and so rather than take a circuitous route, took the direct bus to where he was heading. Rachel lived on the first floor of a double-storey house. Arjun rang the bell and went up the stairs. Rachel opened the door. She was also wearing a white kurta-pyjama. They looked at each other and spontaneously burst out laughing at the similarity of their outfits.

'Well, well,' said Arjun, 'you have certainly adopted Indian ways in the very short time you have been here.'

'When in India, do as the Indians do,' said Rachel. 'Don't you agree? But come in and sit down, we can't talk by the front door all day.'

The furnishings in the room were simple. Arjun made himself comfortable on the large sofa. Rachel brought in two mugs of tea.

'Shekhar tells me you spent many years at Oxford. You were doing a PhD when you left. Why did you come back to India?'

'That's a very long story,' said Arjun. 'Might take a very long time to tell.'

'I have lots of time,' said Rachel. 'And I am all ears.'

'Oxford was my dream,' said Arjun. 'I felt that if I studied and graduated from there, the whole world would open up to me. And it was indeed a dream, but I got seduced by the life and beauty of the place and lost my bearings. I studied hard, but over time I descended into a very decadent way of living. Too much wine, women and song.'

'Many of us go through such a phase in life,' said Rachel. 'One is searching but cannot find an anchor. So there is an aimless and hedonistic drift.'

'Ah! But it wasn't just a phase,' said Arjun. 'I got into a circle that was part of the British aristocracy and most weekends we would end up partying at some country estate or grand country house or the other. It had become a way of life for me. I had even gotten to the point where if I had not been invited to a weekend party, I would try and gatecrash one in London or somewhere in the countryside. I remember once when I was stopped by the doorman of some fancy house in London, I claimed to be a grandee from India.

'"I am the Maharaja of Jodhpur, my dear fellow," I said to the doorman. And he replied, "One moment, sir!" and went off to check whether I was on the invitation list. A few minutes later, he came back with another Indian gentleman sporting a large handlebar moustache. The Indian said, "I don't know who you are, but I am the Maharaja of Jodhpur! So I suggest you get the hell out of here before I call the police!" And then I was summarily thrown out of the premises.

'That's all I did for two years. Pure decadence and hedonism. But then one day I had a vision of myself growing old in England, just a drunken old partygoer who had never achieved anything in life. I saw myself getting my PhD and either continuing to teach and work at Oxford, or joining some big bank in London, and somehow it did not seem to have any meaning.'

'And so you turned to Marxism?' said Rachel. 'I hope you don't mind my saying so, but it sounds as if you needed to believe in something and so you picked this particular worldview, almost like becoming a religious fanatic!'

Arjun liked her directness. 'No, no,' he said. 'It was not like that at all. As a student of Delhi University in the mid 1960s, I was very concerned about the poverty and exploitation I saw around me in India. But at that stage, I was mainly interested in my personal development, and I did not understand much about politics anyway. It was only after I got to Oxford and started reading about the Chinese revolution, and other popular movements around the world, that I began to understand people indeed have the power to bring about social change. But they need to be guided by strong political leadership and a movement that embodies their interests. I think what the Chinese Communist Party did under the leadership of Mao-Tse Tung was incredible. They started as a small group inspired by Marxist–Leninist thinking, and eventually mobilized the people of China to create a new society, one based on equality and freedom from the exploitation of capitalists and landlords. More than anything, that's what influenced me to become a Marxist.'

He looked at her. 'But tell me about yourself. I heard you mention that you had been part of the student protests against authoritarian governments in Europe in 1968.'

'Before I tell you about that, would you like some red wine?' said Rachel. 'I have been given a nice bottle by a friend at the Embassy.'

'Sure,' said Arjun. 'Though I don't drink much any more. The only alcohol I have recently had is tharra, the local brew, with my friends in the Harijan sweeper community.'

Rachel poured out two glasses of wine and then came over to sit next to him on the sofa.

'Paris was the centre of the new consciousness amongst the young in Europe at that time. We were against so much that was repressing us: burdens of the past, the Vietnam War, de Gaulle and his militaristic government, the lack of emancipation of women, restraints on the freedom of expression, and so on. I wanted to be a part of the movement to bring about change, and so I joined the Sorbonne to do my master's degree. And then there was the visit of the Shah of Iran in 1967. I was there at the protests when Benno Ohnesorg, a fellow German student, was shot in the head. That made us all very angry indeed. Subsequently, the movement escalated and in May 1968, millions of workers joined the protests. Street battles were fought with the police all over the country. For a moment, it seemed like a revolutionary government would be formed in France, following in the footsteps of the Paris Commune of 1871. I was a part of the Sorbonne Occupation Committee with Dany le Rouge and others. But then the communists betrayed us. They did not want the violent overthrow of the Gaullist government. After this the movement petered out.'

'Amazing,' said Arjun. 'What a movement that must have been! Students and working people uniting against a repressive state! You must hate the communists then, and have reservations about Marxism as a revolutionary philosophy.'

'I most certainly do,' said Rachel. 'After that experience I read the works of Bakunin, who was critical of Marx and his thinking at that time, and I believe Bakunin's view of the transition from capitalism to socialism is more valid.'

'In what way?' asked Arjun.

'Well, Marx believed that the mechanism of the state should be taken over by the working people led by the communist party, and the state should be used as an instrument of repression to eliminate the feudals, capitalists and other opponents of socialism. However, as Bakunin observed, this was just replacing one dictatorship with another, and eventually the so-called socialist state would also degenerate into a bureaucratic–military elite. This is exactly what happened in the Soviet Union. Bakunin's alternative was that the capitalist state should be replaced with self-governing structures such as communes or revolutionary committees. The establishment of such structures would result in the withering away of state, as we know it – to use Marxist terminology – and bring about a truly democratic form of socialism. For these views, Bakunin was labelled an anarchist. But I don't think there is anything anarchistic about this view.'

Although Arjun was enjoying the conversation and becoming more and more comfortable with Rachel's presence, various thoughts began to flit through his mind. He had left England to find some meaning in his life, and certainly, his participation in radical activities in the past eight or nine months had given him a great sense of satisfaction. He had stayed away from any physical or emotional involvement with a woman because he felt this would be a distraction and divert him from concentrating on his main goals. But by now he had consumed three glasses of red wine and somehow the grand objectives he wanted to achieve seemed far away. What was immediate was a pretty girl who was clearly attracted to him. He reached out and kissed her.

Arjun spent the night with Rachel. But when he woke up early the next morning, he was annoyed and angry with himself. He felt he had allowed the alcohol to dull his senses and drifted into a situation he was not entirely comfortable with. Rachel was still sleeping when he got out of bed, quietly put his clothes on, and slipped out of the house without waking her up or saying goodbye.

During the next few weeks, Arjun returned to his regular activities: writing for the journal, spending time at the printing press correcting proofs for the next issue, participating in workers' study groups, and forming more activist cells amongst the safai karamcharis. He tried, but could not get Rachel out of his mind. He liked her honest, straightforward manner. No emotional games being played there. He enjoyed talking to and being with her. He was now confused. On the one hand, he did not want anything to distract him from his revolutionary endeavours, and yet he felt he was not an obsessive fanatic who could dismiss all emotional interaction for the sake of pursuing some overarching political goal. One didn't have to be exclusively hedonistic, as he had been at Oxford, or a puritanical activist, as he had been for the past nine months, he thought. Surely there could be a balance between the two. He made up his mind. He would see Rachel again. He passed by her flat and left a note saying he would visit her again the following Saturday, and he hoped she would be in. He was of course not sure how she would react to him or whether she would even be at home after his inexplicable disappearance the last time they met.

Saturday arrived and Arjun was at Rachel's doorstep again. She opened the door and looked at him with curiosity. There was no hostility on her face. Arjun was even more confused now. He had expected anger, but there was none. 'May I come in?' he said.

'Sure,' said Rachel. 'Come in and make yourself comfortable.'

Arjun sat on the sofa. Rachel sat opposite him and looked at him earnestly.

'Listen, I am so very sorry about the other day,' he said. 'I really enjoyed every moment with you, but then I began to feel I was slipping back into my old ways and forgetting the whole purpose of my being in India. My commitment to the current movement to bring about social change is absolute and I do not want anything to divert me from this.'

'I fully understand,' said Rachel. 'I admire you for what you are doing and would never dissuade you from doing what you are doing. On the contrary, I would encourage you to wholeheartedly pursue your goal to bring about radical change in India.'

'I know, I know, it's not you. I am the problem,' said Arjun. 'I have to resolve these issues in my own mind.'

'I knew someone else like you once,' said Rachel. 'He was German, a member of the Red Army Faction. His name was Rolf and for a time he was my boyfriend.'

'Red Army Faction!' said Arjun. 'That is the official name of the Baader–Meinhof gang. They are a bunch of terrorists, carrying out kidnappings and killings at random. What were you doing with them?'

'Well, at the time I didn't see them in that light,' said Rachel. 'Rolf introduced me to the ideas of Che Guevara, Régis Debray and Frantz Fanon. Applying Che's strategy during the Cuban revolution to urbanized Europe, Debray advocated the setting up of underground groups that would then undertake urban guerrilla warfare against the state. It seemed to make sense at the time. One of the Red Army activists called Holger Meins even made a short film called *How to Produce a Molotov Cocktail.*'

'You mean you know how to make a Molotov cocktail?' asked Arjun.

'Sure. I made detailed notes. Happy to show you anytime, as long as you have all the right ingredients,' said Rachel, laughing.

'Anyhow, Rolf, my boyfriend, was committed body and soul to the idea of the revolution. He participated in several Red Army bombings and shootings in Germany, and tried to get me to become an activist as well. But I was not convinced about their methods or their goals, and so did not get involved. Eventually, when the police net started closing around the group, he left France some time in 1971 and joined a militant group in the Middle East. I never saw him again. But like you he would appear suddenly and then disappear again, and sometimes I wouldn't see him for months.'

Arjun was irritated. He was being compared to some erratic member of the Red Army Faction in Europe. In his view, they were a bunch of individualistic anarchists who had no philosophy for mobilizing the masses to bring about revolutionary change. They were like the Charu Mazumdar group amongst the Naxalites who believed that individual acts of violence against landlords would inspire the peasantry into mass action against their exploiters.

'I don't think I am like your Baader–Meinhof friend at all. I am not a terrorist,' said Arjun hotly. 'I find that what I am doing at the moment gives me a great deal of satisfaction, and I just don't want anything to distract me or get in the way of the path I am on.'

'As I have already said, I do understand that,' said Rachel. 'But your behaviour the other day was very emotionally distorted. You spent the night with me and then disappeared in the morning without saying a word. Think about it. Schizophrenic behaviour. I am not asking you to change anything in your life or commit to anything. I like you the way you are and we should just enjoy each other's company for so long as our situations converge. How does that sound to you?'

Arjun felt the blood rushing to his face. He had already apologized for his behaviour, and was angry at being told off. But Rachel was being so calm and mature. He felt embarrassed he had behaved in such a juvenile and confused manner. The moment passed. He said, 'Thanks for your understanding. Yes, that is perfect!' Then, quickly changing the subject, he said, 'How about showing me those Molotov cocktail notes?'

'What will you do with a Molotov cocktail once you have learned to put one together without blowing yourself up?' asked Rachel.

Arjun did not like this frivolity. 'Well, I certainly don't intend to use it in some rash act of terrorism, like your Baader–Meinhof friends,' he said. 'Violence is only justifiable as a defence against violence perpetrated by the state, or perhaps in support of a mass movement.'

And so the arguments with Rachel continued into the evening, within the confines of the amicable and affectionate relationship they had now established. Outside, the unrest and people's movement were intensifying. In January that year the Gujarat Nav Nirman or Regeneration movement began under the leadership of Jayaprakash Narayan, the revolutionary Gandhian leader, popularly known as JP. There were statewide strikes of worker and students. More than eighty-five people were killed in police firings. In spite of these harsh measures, the authorities could not cope with the escalating violence. The Gujarat state government was forced to resign, and the army had to be called out to control the situation. Meanwhile, in the eastern part of India, the students of Bihar had set up the Bihar Chhatra Sangharsh Samiti, or the Bihar Students' Struggle Committee. Demonstrations and strikes were becoming a daily occurrence. Soon Arjun would be engulfed in the throes of this struggle. But for now he slept peacefully in the arms of his German lover. He was never to see her again. In the forthcoming days, Arjun became completely immersed in the national railway strike, and by the time this was over, Rachel had left the country for good.

4

Delhi Bandh

ARJUN MET THE VETERAN trade unionist George Fernandes in February 1974. Over the years, the railway workers had continued to suffer various forms of economic injustice. Low pay, irregular hours and temporary employment were only some of the problems they faced. Repeated negotiations with the government had brought little relief. Eventually, their trade union – the All India Railwaymen's Federation – under the leadership of George Fernandes decided that strikes were the only way forward. Meetings were held in the railway colonies all over the country to mobilize the workers. There was a large railway colony in the vicinity of the Swadeshi Mills factory where Arjun was active, and through the factory workers he had come to know many of the railway employees. Arjun attended one of the mobilization meetings held there and addressed by the trade union leadership. Fernandes was a passionate and fiery speaker, and Arjun was immediately attracted to him. After the meeting, the workers introduced

Arjun to George as their local activist, a popular leader and editor of a workers' magazine.

George was intrigued by the young man. He asked, 'What is the name of your magazine? Why don't you join my political party, the Socialist Party, and work with us?'

Arjun had a copy of the latest edition of *Janvaad* in his satchel. He gave this to George. One look at it and George said, 'Ah! So you are a communist, but of which persuasion? I hope you do not belong to the pro-Russian CPI. They have become stooges of Mrs Gandhi's government and essentially are an anti-people party.'

'No,' said Arjun. 'The established communist parties have all sold out. They do not fight the cause of the workers and peasants of India. I have aligned myself with one of the Marxist–Leninist groups – Naxalites in common parlance – but unlike some of them, we believe in bringing about revolutionary change through mass mobilization rather than individual acts of violence.'

'If you believe in mass mobilization, we can work together,' said George. 'As you may know, we are in the process of mobilizing a national railway strike. The idea is to paralyse the country and bring about the collapse of the Congress government. Look at the brutality with which Mrs Gandhi has treated the people's movement in Gujarat. More than 100 people have been killed or injured in police firings. She is a fascist, and is surrounded by a coterie that is determined to destroy India's democratic system. So we are of the view that the time has come to use extra-constitutional means to overthrow the current regime. They are corrupt, dictatorial and brutal.'

Arjun could not agree more with George about his characterization of the Congress government and the need to use all means at one's disposal to bring about its downfall.

'You already know many of our railway activists in this area,' said George. 'Why don't you come over to my flat in the parliamentarians' quarters in New Delhi? We can then discuss how to work together to achieve our common goals. We need to make the strike action being planned a total success.'

Arjun and George shook hands. It was the beginning of a relationship that would last through the dark days of the ensuing Emergency. A few days after they met, Arjun went over to George's flat. Here he was introduced to some of the leaders of the Railwaymen's Federation who were active in the northern region. It was agreed that he and his CPI (ML) activists would travel to various railway colonies around Delhi to generate more fervour, and to mobilize the workers to participate in the strike so that it was a success.

Harsh, Ram Sewak and Arjun spent the next few weeks travelling to various small towns near Delhi where there were concentrations of railway workers. The message they delivered was the same. The railway workers must fight for their economic and political rights. The people of India, from Gujarat to Bihar, were revolting against tyranny and fascism. So they were part of a countrywide movement to bring about a fair and just society. The government of Indira Gandhi must be defeated and dislodged as a first step towards achieving these goals. Faridabad, Ghaziabad, Saharanpur were amongst the many towns they visited. They would arrive at Delhi railway station, meet the local railwaymen's representative, and then board a train for one of these destinations, ticketless, and generally either in the engine cabin or the conductor's room at the rear of the train.

On one of these journeys Arjun took the train to Saharanpur and then all the way to Dehradun. This was the same journey he had taken as a child on the Doon School Express. How different this journey was, he thought. Then, travelling to receive an education at India's most exclusive public school, it would have been expected that he would in due course join the elite of the country. Doon School, St Stephen's College, Oxford University – all these steps pointed towards an expected and well-defined future. Now uncertainty governed his future. He did not know what the next day would bring. His only certainty was his commitment to his cause. Yet, he thought, there was not much difference in a philosophical sense between his condition and that of India as a whole. Historically, India was going through a period of great uncertainty and change as well. That thought comforted him. So in a sense he was only a product of the times, and at least he was aligned with the emergent forces, rejecting the old and corrupt, trying to bring about a new and just society in India.

After his meeting in the railway workers' colony in Dehradun, Arjun took a bus to Doon School. He had no intention of going into his old alma mater. But as he walked past the school's playing fields, he spent some time watching the children practising athletics or playing various sports. How happy and oblivious they were to what the future may bring. After all, he had been one of them some fifteen years ago. He took the night train back to Delhi, this time sleeping soundly in the conductor's carriage.

ON 8 MAY 1974, the national railway strike began. The mobilization was complete and seventeen lakh railway workers stopped work. The entire railway system in India came to a standstill. Railway stations all over the country went quiet; the transport of goods from one part of the country to another ceased.

The strike started off peacefully. The workers stayed at home in their colonies. But the Congress government of Mrs Gandhi was infuriated. They saw this as yet another move by the opposition to cause chaos and make the country ungovernable. No effort was made to call the railway union leaders to the table to discuss their long-standing economic demands and arrive at a solution. Instead, temporary workers were hired and army engineers called out to get the trains moving again. The railway workers reacted angrily to this, and violence broke out along the railway tracks all over the country. Trains were stopped, railway equipment sabotaged, and temporary workers beaten up. The government's response to this was to let loose a reign of terror on the railway workers and their families. Their colonies were attacked by the police and paramilitary forces. Lathi charges and firings occurred in many places, resulting in injury and loss of life.

Arjun and his group of activists had played a key role in mobilizing and obtaining the support of the railway workers in central and western Delhi. They had made the Swadeshi Mills railway colony their base. Using the Molotov cocktail design given to them by Rachel, they had actually experimented in making them and tested some prototypes on an isolated stretch of the Yamuna bank near the university. The cocktails seemed to be quite easy to make and functioned effectively, exploding and spreading their flames once they had been thrown at a target. Harsh had become particularly proficient at making them, lighting them up at the right time and throwing them a good distance with the sweep of his arm. This gained him the nickname 'Major'. He was their artilleryman. They now had a small stock of the cocktails in the railway colony.

Their first action in support of the railway strike occurred a few days after it had started. Some goods trains had restarted their movements. Close to the Swadeshi Mills colony was a mass of railway tracks and crossover points for trains exiting western Delhi. These were all coordinated through a signal control tower nearby. The group decided that if they could render the tower non-functional, that would prevent any train movements from Delhi. Late one night Harsh and a group of railway workers cautiously made their way to the tower. It was a dark and moonless night. There was no one in the signal tower. That made the operation easy. They entered the tower, spread petrol all over the levers, switches and other control equipment, and then stepped outside. Harsh then lit a Molotov cocktail and tossed it into the cabin. The entire tower caught fire, and the group quickly retreated into the darkness. No trains could be heard passing through this track junction in the ensuing days. The burning down of the railway tower, however, enraged the authorities. In the following week, without any warning, the Swadeshi Mills railway colony was attacked by a huge force of police and paramilitary soldiers. They mercilessly beat up anyone they could lay their hands on. Even women and children were not spared. The known leaders of the strike who lived in the colony were rounded up and arrested. Their families were evicted from their houses, and all their household belongings were thrown out on to the streets. Arjun and his friends were not present in the colony when this attack happened, so they escaped being beaten up and arrested. But after this event, they could not venture back into the area due to the continued and significant police presence. The remaining Molotov cocktails were never retrieved or used.

IN SUPPORT OF THE railway strike, and to protest against the reign of terror unleashed by the government, the opposition alliance decided to organize a Delhi bandh. The railway strike had been continuing for about ten days now, and in spite of the severe repression, it showed no signs of abating. Arjun and his group felt this would be an excellent opportunity to mobilize industrial workers in support of the railway strike, foster worker solidarity, and show the government that the masses in the capital city were against their anti-people economic policies and repressive behaviour. Early morning on the day of the bandh, a small group of CPI (ML) activists entered the Wazirpur industrial estate. The area consisted of fifty or more small factories with thirty to fifty workers each. The activists approached the first factory gate and banged on it with their lathis. The workers within responded with shouts of '*Inquilab zindabad!*', and before the management or guards could react, threw open the front gates, declared a strike, and walked out of the factory premises. A similar succession of events at all the Wazirpur factories soon resulted in a crowd of over 1,000 workers coming out on to the streets.

The procession now wound its way towards Birla Mills, stopping traffic and making sure that any shops that were still open were closed immediately. At Birla Mills, the activist cells consisting of the purabias from eastern UP were already on alert, awaiting the procession from Wazirpur. As soon as it arrived at the gates of the mill, shouts went up from inside, and workers downed tools from one section to the next, streaming out of the factory to join the procession. Now there were more than 5,000 people in the demonstration. This gave Arjun and the others who were leading the march greater courage to continue through the old city. Soon, they arrived at the gates of the Swadeshi Mills factory. After the previous strike there, the management was not in any mood to confront this group again, so even before the workers started to down tools and stage a walkout, the close-of-shift whistle was blown to signify that the factory was closed for the day. Many more workers now joined the march. The procession had now swelled to several kilometres long, with many supporters of JP's movement and opposition political groups also joining in.

The air was rent with fiery slogans.

'*Indira Gandhi murdabad!*'

'*Inquilab zindabad!*'

'*Hamari maangen poori karo!*' (Our demands must be met!)

'*Railway strike zindabad!*'

The procession now entered New Delhi and went around the central shopping area of Connaught Place with all its posh shops and eating places. On seeing the huge crowd of demonstrators, the owners of the establishments quickly pulled down their shutters. It was late afternoon by the time the procession entered Parliament Street. Up to this point, they had not been confronted by any police presence. However, Arjun and the others knew that if they went further towards the Parliament building there would undoubtedly be barricades and a strong force of police or paramilitary troops present to stop and disperse the crowd. So far, it had not been clear what the end objective of this march was except to mobilize the workers, make the Delhi bandh a success, and show the government that the people of Delhi were in full support of the railway workers. In this, the organizers felt they had already succeeded. Shops and factories had been closed, traffic brought to a standstill, and thousands of people from the ordinary public encouraged to join the protest. Within the procession, there were several groups of activists who were carrying red paint. This had been used to write anti-government and workers' solidarity slogans on walls all along the way, particularly in the New Delhi area. There had been no clashes or violence so far.

After a quick consultation amongst the protest leaders at the head of the procession, it was agreed that it would be counter-productive to try to attack the Parliament building itself. After all, Parliament was a symbol of democracy, and in fact, it was the current Congress government that was doing its best to undermine democratic processes and create an authoritarian state. So it was agreed that ideally, if they could approach the Parliament building and write their slogans all over it, this would not only a fitting finale to the Delhi bandh protest but would also show the government that the people had no fear about coming into the heart of New Delhi, the seat of government, to express their anger.

BY NOW, THE MARCHERS were quite close to the Parliament building, and the police barricades and policemen behind them were clearly visible. About 20 yards separated the marchers from the security personnel. From behind the barricades, a senior police officer with pips on his shoulders came out with a loudhailer.

He said, 'You are in contravention of Section 144 of the Criminal Procedure Code. Section 144 has been declared in this area and no gathering of more than five people is permitted. I am therefore ordering you to disperse immediately.'

The protest organizers were ready for this. Activists started moving crowds of people into the buildings on either side of Parliament Street. Another group took several thousand protesters down a side road so that they were now situated to the left side of the police barricades directly in front of them. The police commanders were not happy with these movements and the megaphone came out again. The Section 144 message and order to disperse was repeated.

Now Arjun and his group played their trump card. They brought out Ram Chander, an ex-policeman and a well-known leader of the Provincial Armed Constabulary (PAC) of Uttar Pradesh. The PAC had mutinied and gone on strike in May 1973 to protest against poor pay and conditions of service. Ram Chander took a loudhailer and walked up to stand in front of the protestors. He said, 'My name is Ram Chander. Like you I am a policeman. I was part of the UP-PAC strike last year and was dismissed from service for my participation in that action. We are all brothers! You are all poorly paid and exploited by the government of Indira Gandhi. So you are in the same situation as me and the thousands of our brother workers who are protesting here against the economic hardships we all face. We have no fight with you. In fact, we are fighting for you and your rights.'

The police personnel looked uncertain at this intervention. There were only about 200 of them and the crowds looked menacing. There were thousands of protestors, many armed with sticks and staves, perhaps other weaponry, who surrounded them on several fronts. It was the 1970s, and at that time, police battalions were armed with lathis, old .303 Enfield rifles, and some tear gas. Effective enough armaments against unarmed protestors, but this crowd looked different: militant, fearless and threatening.

Ram Sewak now came out in front and took the megaphone. He said, 'My brothers, as my friend Ram Chander has said, we have no fight with you. All we want to do is show the government our anger and our support for the railway workers' demands. We do not want to attack the Parliament buildings. We will stay where we are. All we want is for you to let a group of us pass through to Parliament so we can paint our slogans on the walls there. Once this is done we will all disperse. Our leaders are now going to approach your commanding officer to show our brotherhood and goodwill.'

At this Ram Chander, Harsh, Arjun, Ram Sewak and a few others crossed over the 20 yards separating the protestors from the barricades and addressed the police officers. Arjun now spoke. He said, 'Brothers, if you allow us to finish what we want to do and then disperse peacefully, the authorities will congratulate you for preventing an attack on Parliament by a dangerous mob. We can then all go home happily to our families and have dal-roti for supper. A little bit of paint on the walls of Parliament will be excused by your bosses.' The ice was broken. Many of the policemen started laughing. The commanding officers said nothing. Arjun then beckoned to the activists carrying paint. They walked over to the walls of Parliament and wrote out all their slogans. Their task completed, the crowd gradually began to disperse. The Delhi bandh had been a success and there had been no incidents of violence.

Elsewhere, however, the reign of terror let loose by the government continued unabated. During the next two weeks, over 50,000 railway workers were arrested and imprisoned. Entire families of railway union activists and leaders were evicted from their homes. Eventually, the workers could take no more and the strike was withdrawn after twenty-two days on 28 May 1974. The government declared the withdrawal of the strike to be a great victory over the forces of chaos and darkness. However, it had been an unparalleled experience for the working classes. The railway strike of 1974 was the largest-ever industrial action in India. By using brute force to crush it, Mrs Gandhi's government had shown its true fascist character. State-sponsored violence was being used extensively to suppress any protest movement by the people. The government talked of poverty reduction and socialism while practising dictatorial and anti-people policies. The CPI (ML) in Delhi was pleased with itself. Their tactics and advance organization during the Delhi bandh had paid off. Their reputation amongst the working classes of Delhi had risen. Going forward, their ability and success in mobilizing the people for social action would be much easier.

5

The Bhangi of Seelampur

THE SUCCESS OF THE Delhi bandh and the role played by the CPI (ML) in mobilizing the workers attracted further attention from the authorities towards the activities of Arjun's group. His brother's house was now under almost continuous surveillance and he was never quite sure when a police raid or arrest may occur. His political activities were also putting his brother's family at the risk of reprisals from the state. Arjun therefore decided to move permanently to Seelampur, the large Harijan colony in Shahdara. To finalize this arrangement, he spoke to Shankar dada. Shankar was an elder of the community and had been quite a revolutionary in his younger days. Over seventy years old, he was tall, sported pince-nez glasses, and always wore a white kurta and dhoti. He had passionately supported Mahatma Gandhi, and thirty years ago had participated in the Quit India movement. Throughout his life, he had been a Congress supporter. But over the years, he had seen atrocity upon atrocity being committed on his community by the upper castes, and the government had always stood by passively, never defending the rights of the lower castes. So now, like many others in his community, he had grown disenchanted with the Congress, and was inspired by the left-wing ideas of the Naxalites.

Shankar lived alone and had an extra room in his hut. He told Arjun it would be a great honour if he lived there. Thus, Arjun became a resident of Seelampur. The colony was characterized by the filth and squalor found in most of these slums. The pathways were narrow and unpaved, with open gutters on either side. In the monsoon season, the gutters could not cope with the rainwater and raw sewage would overflow on to the pathways. There was no piped water supply. A few boreholes existed from which water was pumped out using handpumps. Illegal electric connections had been tapped from the transmission lines that passed through the colony. This provided lighting in some of the huts. Scantily clothed children ran around the area, shouting, screaming and playing noisily with homemade toys made out of wires and the caps of fizzy drinks. The colony had pigs galore. They were large, black and hairy, with piglets of different sizes following the adults around, squeaking and squealing loudly. The pigs spent most of their time rummaging in the rubbish and filth that was plentiful in the area, eating whatever they could find. A particularly delicious mouthful would be a pile of fresh human faeces deposited on a pathway by some child who could not be bothered to visit the public toilets. Between the pigs and the children, Seelampur was a noisy place.

Food was not a problem. Shanker's meals would come from his daughter, who lived nearby. If Arjun were around, he would join him for the meal. Otherwise, he could just wander over to Ram Sewak's hut and Angoori would cook him something. The fare was always simple: thick rotis made out of wheat or coarse grains like bajra and jowar, and dal or some sabzi. For his morning tea, Arjun would wander over to the chaiwala on the main road close by. Here he would be given a large glass of steaming hot milky tea and a sweet bun. That would get him started for the day. Once a week the chaiwala also made jalebis. Arjun would make sure he never missed this occasion. The jalebis would be submerged in a glass of hot milk and then slowly pried out piece by piece and eaten as if they were the ultimate gourmet dish. Sometimes, while eating the jalebis, Arjun would reminisce about his days at Doon School, when he would enjoy much the same experience at chaiwala shops in the Himalayan foothills. Quite a change of scene, though, from those lofty mountains to the dusty and traffic-infested main highway in Shahdara that connected Delhi to Uttar Pradesh.

At the chai shop, Arjun came across the rickshaw pullers of Shahdara. East Delhi had more than 1,000 rickshaw-walas. Most of them were from eastern UP and Bihar, and had been plying this trade for many years, earning a few rupees a day and eking out a miserable existence for themselves and their families. They were not allowed to enter New Delhi, but could carry passengers and goods across the Yamuna into Chandni Chowk and other parts of Old Delhi. Arjun would watch these thin men, their bodies almost just skin and bone, carrying three or four passengers at a time, or large loads of goods, on their tricycles. He would wonder how they had the strength to pedal such huge weights, day after day. In talking to them at the chai shop, he discovered they had many problems. This included harassment and confiscation of their rickshaws by the police for any small infringement of the traffic laws, complex application procedures, and high road licence fees of the municipality. He decided to help them. As a first step, he proposed that they form a rickshaw-pullers' union. A meeting was held, which was attended by twenty rickshaw-walas, and the union was set up. Appropriate forms were obtained from the municipality and the union was registered with the Delhi administration. Its registered office was the chai shop. Arjun did not want to play too prominent a role in the new union. He was already feeling very exposed after the Delhi bandh. So he encouraged the union functionaries to play a leading role in all activities while continuing to help them with their paperwork and petitions, and advising them in private.

The first action the union undertook was to petition the municipality to give automatic road licences to any person who filled in the application form and produced a rickshaw as proof that he was indeed a rickshaw-wala. It was also demanded that the licence fee be fixed at 10 rupees per annum. A demonstration was planned to support these demands at the local municipal office. On the specified day, almost every single rickshaw-wala in east Delhi pedalled over to the municipal offices, blocking all the roads that led to it and creating a barricade on the main Delhi–Uttar Pradesh highway. The authorities were dismayed at this show of strength by the rickshaw-pullers. There were not even enough policemen in the area to control or disperse this demonstration. The head of the East Delhi municipal office had no choice but to come out and meet the petitioners. He accepted the petition, expressed his sympathy with the demands, and promised to consult his head office to get a quick answer. Two weeks later, the rickshaw union was informed in writing that the road licence fee had been reduced to 10 rupees per annum. After this success, the rickshaw-pullers became friends and couriers of the CPI (ML). Arjun and other activists could get a free rickshaw ride to any part of east or Old Delhi. During the Emergency, this help became invaluable. The rickshaw-pullers could be trusted to carry messages, or even packages of anti-government literature, to activists in other parts of the city. The police could never have imagined that these impoverished rickshaw-walas were functioning as couriers for the revolution.

IT WAS EARLY WINTER. Arjun had been living in Seelampur for the past few months. He was now well known in the community, and of course spent a considerable amount of time with the youths of the Krantikari Harijan Sangh. A study circle would be held once a week, starting in the evening and continuing late into the night. Young men from the other safai karamchari colonies all over Delhi had become regular visitors, and through them, the CPI (ML) extended its influence over most of the slum areas of the city. Ram Sewak, Harsh and Arjun began to hold regular meetings and study groups in jhuggi-jhompri areas such as Ajmeri Gate, Karol Bagh and as far as the old fortress of Tughlakabad. In spite of this close association, however, Arjun never really felt he was a part of the Harijan community until the wedding of Angoori's sister.

Winter had started, and with it the wedding season in Delhi. Angoori's sister Chameli was to wed another member of the community, but one who had had the good fortune of graduating from a municipal sweeper into a chaprasi, or messenger, in a government office. This was a very important position, since chaprasis controlled the access to more senior officials in government offices. Members of the public trying to meet government officials had therefore to treat them with respect. The wedding was to be held in a small open field in the middle of Seelampur. A small pandal had been erected for the bride and bridegroom to sit under during the wedding ceremony. A few old carpets and straw mats had been laid out in front of the pandal. To add to the greenery, boughs and branches from trees had been cut and stuck into the ground around the field. A few strings of fairy lights had been draped over the cut branches to give the area an atmosphere of festivity. Apart from these few decorations the only other indication that a wedding was to be held were the large steel cooking pots on one side of the field, where the food for the event was being cooked on open fires. In accordance with the importance of this occasion, several pigs had been slaughtered and pork would be served to the guests today as a delicacy.

It was early in the evening when the bridegroom arrived with the usual fanfare. Given his status as a government chaprasi, he could afford to ride in on a horse, followed by a band playing raucous music. Members of his entourage, the baraat, followed the band, dancing and gesticulating wildly to show their full involvement in this joyous occasion. As the procession entered the field, they were joined by scores of locals from the colony itself. The bride, her head covered in a veil, was waiting in front of the pandal to welcome the bridegroom. It was not quite clear who was going to conduct the wedding ceremony, since it was unlikely that a Brahmin priest would be willing to venture into this lower-caste gathering. But then out of the procession emerged a person dressed in kurta-pyjama who took charge of the ceremony. Arjun later discovered he was an official of the Arya Samaj movement, a progressive Hindu sect that did not believe in the caste system and was actively campaigning for an abolition of this pernicious system of social discrimination. Soon the wedding ceremony was over and food was served.

Arjun was sitting on a low stool on one side of the field with Shankar dada. He was given a steel plate with pork curry, roasted sweet potatoes and thick rotis. Looking at the curry, he thought it likely that the meat came from the same pigs he saw every day eating human faeces and other filth off the streets of Seelampur. All very well integrating with the Harijan community, but he didn't really think he could stomach this stuff. He looked around and found that everyone else was voraciously digging into their food. Shankar dada glanced sideways and saw that Arjun had not touched his food. He said, 'What's the matter, don't you like our food?'

Arjun did not know what to say. He was embarrassed and confused. Shankar dada then smiled and said, 'It's the pig meat, isn't it? You haven't ever eaten anything like this before and you find it disgusting to eat the flesh of these filthy animals. Well, let me tell you that you are not alone. During the Independence movement, there were many upper-caste followers of Mahatma Gandhi who worked closely with our community, but when it came to eating the flesh of pigs that roamed around in our colonies, they could not cope with the idea. They would pretend to be vegetarians to avoid any embarrassment on this issue!'

'But let me reassure you,' Shankar dada continued, 'there is nothing unhygienic about the meat. Think about all the vegetables and plants we eat. They are fertilized using manure from animals and solid waste from the sewage treatment works in the city. The plants only absorb the good nutrients and produce healthy food for us. It is the same with the pigs. Besides, the meat has been cooked for the past twelve hours, with our own special spices, and it is very tasty. So, beta, do taste it at least.'

Arjun had no more excuses. He took a chunk of meat from his plate and put it in his mouth. He was pleasantly surprised. It turned out to be soft and juicy, with the spices giving it a tangy taste. All his doubts disappeared and he quickly wolfed down the pork curry and rotis.

NOW A DRUMMER EMERGED in front of the wedding pandal. It was time for dancing. The revellers gathered around the drummer and encouraged him to accelerate his beat. The girls of the community joined in, forming their own small circles, twirling their ghagras and jangling their thick plastic bangles. Arjun was still sitting next to Shankar dada and enjoying being an observer rather than an active participant. He was now offered a cup with some milky looking substance in it. He thought it was the usual kheer that one is served as part of a north Indian meal. He took a sip, but it tasted different. Shankar dada looked at him and smiled again. 'It is not kheer,' he said, reading Arjun's thoughts. 'It is bhang.'

'Bhang!' Arjun stuttered. 'Bhang!'

'Sure,' said Shankar dada. 'Haven't you had bhang during Holi? It is quite normal for bhang to be offered to visitors who come to your house during the festival period. In our community, it is traditional to imbibe bhang during festive events such as weddings or religious occasions. As an intoxicant, I much prefer it to alcohol, the favourite drink of the rich. Alcohol makes one aggressive. Bhang on the other hand calms you down and mellows you. All human beings start looking beautiful. And then, at the end of it all, you have a deep and dreamless sleep.'

Arjun thought about this. He had never consumed bhang before, but it was just an extract from the cannabis plant. He had tried marijuana once when he was holidaying in Morocco. It was called kif there. He and his English friend had wandered into one of the numerous cafés which surrounded the souk in Tangiers. The air was thick with a sweet-smelling smoke. They had ordered the local green tea made with mint leaves. As they sipped the sweet, spicy tea, a pipe filled with marijuana was passed around the table. Everyone in the café seemed to be smoking the stuff, so Arjun and his friend accepted the pipe and enjoyed a few puffs of the kif, interspersed with sips of sweet mint tea. The tea over, they wandered onto the nearby beach and sat there watching the rhythmic movement of the waves. Arjun's most distinct memory was that the Mediterranean Sea before him had taken on an exceptionally bright blue hue. He was sure this was the effect of the marijuana they had smoked.

That was all that he could remember of that experience, but it had certainly been a very pleasant afternoon.

So Arjun thought that if the bhang was anything like that marijuana, it should not be too bad. Besides, if he wanted to be fully accepted as part of the Harijan sweeper community, he must go along with their traditions. Without thinking further, he downed the cup of bhang. Soon the drums began to sound louder, the drum beat more frenetic. He turned to look at Shankar dada. How odd, he thought, Shankar's smile looked like that of the Cheshire Cat in *Alice in Wonderland*! He heard some grunts behind him. Five or six piglets were scrounging around for food. As he looked at them, though, they turned into funny little creatures with pointy snouts, wing-like ears and twirly tails! More creatures, this time from *Through the Looking Glass*, he thought. What were they doing wandering around in Seelampur? He rubbed his eyes vigorously and looked again. The piglets had regained the form of piglets. That was reassuring.

The drumming was getting louder and drew Arjun's attention to the revellers dancing in small groups. How beautiful the women looked in their skimpy, backless cholis, swirling ghagras and arms laden with bangles. He was mesmerized by their rhythmic movements. Then suddenly the scene changed. He wasn't hearing drum beats any more. The music was that of the Rolling Stones with Mick Jagger screaming,

> *I cain't get no satisfaction, I cain't get no satisfaction*
> *'Cause I try and I try and I try and I try*
> *I cain't get no, I cain't get no…*

He was back in Oxford rocking the dance floor with Judith, one of his many girlfriends. Such a lovely girl Judith was.

So warm, intelligent, with progressive views, and an ardent feminist. She had been Miss Oxford as well. They had dated for about six months, but then she had broken it off since she had found Arjun to be a charmer but reactionary and chauvinistic in his thinking.

Yes, he did remember – that's how he used to be. Reactionary and chauvinistic. But being dumped by Judith had shaken his confidence in himself, his worldview and who indeed he really was. It began a process of introspection and study that lasted the rest of his time at Oxford. He began to see that the life was not just about focusing on oneself and one's selfish needs. Other people mattered, and the world was full of greed, discrimination and oppression. It was this process that eventually led him to where he was today.

In the midst of this reverie, Arjun looked around. He was back in Seelampur now, standing by the dancers. But his feet were not moving. There was no Judith any more, and the revellers in front of him started to look like shadows swaying to the drumbeat. He tried to move but his feet had become leaden and heavy. Shankar dada could see that Arjun was hallucinating and acting strangely. He took him by the hand and led him back to his hut. Arjun lay down on the charpai. His last thought before he fell asleep brought a smile to his face and made him feel proud. He had indeed become a Bhangi of Seelampur. His integration with the working classes was now complete.

WHILE ARJUN CONTINUED TO mobilize the Harijans of Seelampur and other areas of Delhi, the unrest in the country and the anger against Mrs Gandhi's regime intensified. On 3 October 1974, Jayaprakash Narayan called for a Bihar-wide strike against the state government. Demonstrations were held all over the state, and clashes between the agitators and the police became widespread. The Bihar Chhatra Sangharsh Samiti now accused the state government of Bihar of corruption and misgovernance, and demanded that it resign. Mrs Gandhi was in a quandary, but in the face of this huge popular uprising had no choice but to ask JP to come over to Delhi and discuss the people's demands with her. JP stuck to his guns and demanded the resignation of the state government. Mrs Gandhi did not agree to this, fearing that if she did, similar movements would be encouraged in other states where her party held power. The talks broke down.

As a protest against the intransigence of the government and its unwillingness to accede to the people's demands, another rally was called in Patna. There was a massive response to this call, and in early November, a huge rally with over a million people was held in the city. The mood of the people was clear. At this rally, JP advocated that the people's struggle should not just be restricted to Bihar, but extended to the entire country. Again, some of the more progressive elements within the Congress Party tried to broker a deal between JP and Mrs Gandhi. However, this time, the new group in the Congress coalescing around Sanjay Gandhi ensured that no peace deal occurred.

Sanjay Gandhi was the new rising star in the Congress Party. Through reactivating the Youth Congress, he had formed his own power base in the party. In 1974, the Youth Congress, under his leadership, commenced a massive countrywide recruitment drive. By August 1974, three million members had been recruited and a massive rally and youth convention were held in Delhi. Sanjay portrayed himself as a man of action. His longest speech was not more than five minutes. To form the nucleus of the Youth Congress, he had recruited many young and ambitious men and women of the upper middle classes, people of similar social origin and education as him. Several of his ex-Doon School classmates had joined him in what he portrayed as his youth crusade. Through his political network, and from the intelligence reports to which he had access, he discovered that Arjun, yet another one of his classmates, was politically very active amongst the workers and slum dwellers in Delhi. Sanjay decided that he needed someone like Arjun on his side. His current inner circle, though ardently loyal and enthusiastic, lacked experience in mobilizing the people. On the other hand, Arjun had played a major role in the Swadeshi textile mill strike and the Delhi bandh earlier in the year. He decided to reach out to Arjun and call him in for a chat.

It was now January 1975. Mrs Gandhi's popularity was waning. The Congress Party had just lost several by-elections in Madhya Pradesh and Haryana. Sanjay, through one of the university lecturers who was a member of the Youth Congress, sent a message to Arjun to come over to an apartment that he frequented in central Delhi. Arjun had mixed feelings when he received the message. He remembered Sanjay from his Doon School days. The boy had been nasty, arrogant and a bully. He particularly remembered the slap he had once received from Sanjay, one night at school, as a consequence of a silly argument. He could almost feel that hit tingling on his face right now. Sanjay, the spoilt brat, he thought. They were poles apart, nothing in common, so why should he bother going to see him? And yet, he felt a strong sense of curiosity. It was increasingly obvious that Sanjay was the power behind the throne. Senior politicians and ministers in the government were taking directions from him. So perhaps he would learn something about the state of mind in the current government, and how they were intending to react to the wave of unrest in the country. And besides, it was odd that Sanjay would want to meet him after all these years. He could not understand what

Sanjay could possibly want from him. So he made up his mind to go and meet him.

It was a wintry Delhi evening with fog gathering on the streets when Arjun arrived at the address he had been given. The apartment was a penthouse on the top floor of a posh multi-storeyed apartment block owned by a prominent Delhi businessman. Arjun wrapped his woollen shawl tightly around himself and entered the lift to the top floor. The penthouse had a small landing with a large carved wooden entrance door to the apartment. Arjun rang the bell. The door was opened by Sanjay Gandhi, also clad in a white kurta-pyjama with a shawl draped around him.

'Hello, Arjun,' said Sanjay. 'Long time. Come in and take a seat.'

Arjun smiled cautiously at his old classmate and walked in. A couple of other ex-Doon School boys were also there. Vishwas, the obnoxious prefect who had once threatened to beat him up with a cricket bat back in school, was present. They all greeted him with nods. The room had an unusual layout. They were on the upper level, where a number of sofas and other seating arrangements had been set out. Thick satin curtains were draped on the doors and windows. Further down, the room had a lower level, with a small amphitheatre and a stage. Arjun looked at this curiously.

Sanjay, following his gaze, said, 'You like the design of the room? I don't really live here, you know. I use this apartment for entertainment and to relax. That's a dance floor if I have a party. But it can also be used as a stage for a singing troupe or mujrah, which I and my friends can view from up here.'

Arjun thought that this was all a bit degenerate and strange. He felt that the room reeked of decadence, but he did not say anything.

'Would you like a drink perhaps? Whisky-soda, or maybe a brandy to warm you up?' asked Sanjay. Arjun declined politely. Sanjay then continued. 'Let's get on with the topic of today. Arjun, you have become quite a celebrity in certain circles. You came back from Oxford last year and boldly jumped into the political fray. I have been reading some interesting intelligence reports about you. Impressive!'

Arjun was not sure whether Sanjay was being sarcastic or not. He said, 'If you have been reading intelligence reports, then you know I am not a friend of the Congress. On the contrary, I strongly believe in the need for a social and political revolution in India, one that liberates the energies of the people and creates a new and dynamic society.'

'Of course we need a social and political revolution in India,' said Sanjay. 'The question is how this can be brought about. Look at the people of India, mired in religious custom, breeding like rabbits, no vision for a greater tomorrow. Look at your own work over the past year or so. Without your leadership, the poor, lower castes and other workers would still be in deep slumber. That shows the social revolution can only be brought about from the top by a strong and determined leadership, with a clear vision, that leads the country out of the mess we are in.'

'But Sanjay, we are a democracy,' said Arjun. 'The whole idea is that the people should have a voice and be able to influence their own future. Our role as leaders is to help them find that voice, and to mobilize them so that they can achieve economic and political freedoms.'

'Rubbish,' said Sanjay. 'Democracy is a luxury that we can ill afford. Democracy is not a viable system for a poor country. All it does is enable the emergence of disruptive people and parties, which confuses the masses and blocks economic and social progress. Anyway, since when have you become a defender of democracy? Your current political ideology is to overthrow the democratic system in India and replace it with a socialist state. So at least we both agree that democracy is not a viable option for India.'

Arjun decided that arguing with Sanjay would not get him anywhere. So he just said, 'Well, you have a point. But what do you want of me?'

'Look,' said Sanjay, 'the youth of India are yearning for change. I have begun to mobilize them under the banner of the Youth Congress. The organization now has a membership of over four million activists. Imagine what we could achieve if we could provide them with the right guidance and leadership. I have lots of ideas, but I need people like you to work by my side. You are my old schoolmates, people who understand me, people I can trust.

'Besides,' continued Sanjay in a more threatening manner, 'think of what you are doing now, and the prospects going forward. One of these days, the government is going to take a much tougher line against the continuing agitations and disruptions caused by the opposition and your Naxalite crowd. You will end up in jail. It won't help you achieve your goals if you rot in jail for the next two or three years. So join me, and let's make a difference. What do you say?'

Arjun wanted to tell Sanjay off, tell him that all his ideas were politically distasteful, that he and his group were leading his mother, the Prime Minister, in the wrong direction, and that India would lurch into a major historical crisis if they persisted in their ways. But he knew Sanjay's mentality well. To say any of this would only result in extreme hostility and aggression. There was nothing to be gained from such a confrontation. So he said, 'All this is a lot to absorb in an evening. Let me think about it and I will get back to you.'

Sanjay looked irritated at this response. He said, 'That's fine, but there really isn't much time. Our movement is going to surge forward like a deluge and change the face of India. Either you are with us or against us. So make up your mind fast. Come join the leadership of the future. You will not get such an opportunity again.'

Arjun exited the multi-storeyed building and found a taxi on the main road to take him back to Harsh's flat at the university. He was feeling most disturbed by his conversation with Sanjay. He had a horrible sense of foreboding about the future. If Sanjay became a dominant force in Indian politics, terrible things were likely to be perpetrated on the people of India, and certainly the democratic system as it existed at the moment would be at an end. After this conversation, he felt that he must redouble his efforts to mobilize the working classes in Delhi to oppose the oncoming darkness. He never met Sanjay Gandhi again.

6

26 June 1975

IT WAS A LITTLE after midnight on 25 June 1975. Just another hot summer evening in south Delhi. A warm breeze wafted over the rooftops. The party was in full swing on the second-floor terrace garden. Bodies were swaying to the beat of a popular seductive number of the time.

'When a man loves a woman...' the singer crooned.

Sundeep, an up-and-coming marketing executive at a five-star hotel chain, organized such events regularly for the young and the fashionable of Delhi high society. Delicate finger snacks were being served, and of course, the alcohol was flowing.

The conversation was typical of such gatherings. There was apprehension that the current heatwave would get even worse until the predicted pre-monsoon showers arrived. Temperatures were expected to reach over 45 degrees. Anu, the daughter of a prominent industrialist, was describing the new bungalow her father had just purchased in the nearby hill station of Mussoorie.

'It's quite out of this world,' she said. 'Old wooden floors, stone chimneys, and of course, a full view of the snowy

Himalayan peaks in the distance. Our family will be spending the rest of the summer there.'

Not to be outdone, Sheila, the daughter of a senior official in the Prime Minister's Office, indicated that she was off to London for a holiday. 'My brother works for an investment bank and lives just off Hampstead Heath. I shall be able to continue my exercise regime and go jogging on the Heath every day,' she said.

They prattled on, completely self-involved. Cocooned in their rich and comfortable lives, oblivious to the extreme poverty and squalor that surrounded them. The social and political turmoil of the last few years seemed more of an inconvenience than a matter of grave concern for the children of the elite gathered here.

There was one person at the party who seemed to be quite out of place. He was dressed in a slightly crumpled kurta-pyjama and had stubble on his face. Looking at his thick mop of black hair and piercing black eyes, it would have been easy to classify him as another one of those intense young men who worked for some do-good non-governmental organization. Arjun was a school friend of Sundeep's. They had known each other ever since they had been kids, studying together at Doon School. Their lives had moved in different directions, but they had kept in touch with each other from time to time. Arjun had met Sundeep at a friend's house recently and had been invited to this party.

'Don't take yourself so seriously,' Sundeep had said. 'Come to the party, meet some new people, and have some fun.' So Arjun had come. He was not happy, though. He found the people superficial and the conversation vacuous. Though a member of India's upper class himself, this was not his chosen milieu any more. He was therefore sitting on his own, sipping a beer and staring at the gathered crowd in a somewhat hostile manner.

His reverie was broken by a pretty young thing. 'Hello, I am Sheila. Sundeep tells me you are a revolutionary!' she said flippantly with a look of amusement on her face.

'Not really,' said Arjun coldly. 'I am just a political activist.'

By now, a small crowd had gathered to watch the fun. Arjun felt he was being made into an object of ridicule, but he kept calm. 'Political activist?' said Anu, joining in the conversation. 'What kind? Congress, RSS or perhaps communist? Come on, tell us what you really do!'

'Well,' said Arjun, 'India is a poor country. The majority of the people live in intense poverty, and their condition has not improved since Independence almost thirty years ago. So I believe there needs to be a fundamental change in the economic and political system, a revolutionary change.'

'Yes, yes, we all know that,' said Anu. 'This is what Mrs Gandhi and all the other politicians have been saying for years. How about telling us something new? What's so different about what you do?'

'As I said, we need a revolutionary change, like those that happened in Russia and China, where the workers and peasants were mobilized to overthrow the capitalist state, get rid of the landlords and capitalists, and establish their own government. I am an activist working towards that goal. I guess that's what makes me different from all the corrupt and self-seeking bourgeois politicians you are referring to.'

'Aha! So you *are* a commie,' said Sheila. 'But of what kind? There are so many varieties to choose from nowadays. We have the right-wing communists – the CPI, the left-wing communists – the CPI (M), and then of course the extreme, extreme left, the Naxalites.' With some mirth in her voice Sheila continued, 'Are you a Naxalite, by any chance?' She was referring to the new communist group that openly advocated an armed rebellion against the government.

Arjun did not answer. He felt it was pointless to continue this conversation. Then, someone with a glass of Scotch and soda in his hand said, 'You know, the real problem is that the poor are just lazy. Indians believe in karma, and so do nothing to improve their own situation in life. What they need is discipline and the danda. You commie types will never understand this and so you get nowhere.'

Arjun felt his anger rising. Typical middle-class view, he thought. The poor were poor because they were lazy and stupid, but Mr Scotch-in-hand was a rising star because he was smart and hard-working. But it wouldn't get him anywhere if he got into an argument. So he did not say anything.

After this exchange, the pretty young things and the rising executives all lost interest in Arjun. They reverted to drinking, dancing and chatting amongst themselves. Arjun was left to nurse his beer on his own. A little while later, though, Sheila extricated herself from the dance floor, and with a very thin young woman in tow, came over to where Arjun was sitting.

'Hey, don't be offended,' she said. 'We were all just having a bit of fun. Now look at me. I finished my bachelor's degree from Delhi University last year, but I don't really know what I want to do. So for now, I am just sitting at home and doing nothing, fending off efforts by my parents to get me married. But I do have a social conscience, so you must not tar us all with the same brush. Anyhow, I do have to leave now, but I live close by, so come and visit me one of these days. I am off to London for two months, but will be around after that. So if your busy schedule permits, come by.' She smiled sweetly at Arjun and gave him her phone number and address. 'By the way, this is Jyoti,' she said.

'Just met her. She is a social worker like you. Someone with a conscience, a big conscience!'

Arjun now looked at Sheila more carefully. She was very pretty. Grey eyes, light-brown curly hair, alabaster skin and a clear complexion. A few years ago, he would have enthusiastically pursued this conversation with her. He began reminiscing about his days at Oxford. There, such events were his forte and almost his daily fare. He had been an avid partygoer, grabbing centre stage on the dance floor and chatting up the prettiest girls in the crowd. No more of that now, he thought, those hedonistic days were gone. No more Sheilas in his life. He had more important things to do.

Sheila got up and left. But Jyoti remained sitting next to him. He was wondering whether he should also leave the party when Jyoti said, 'I was looking at you from across the terrace when you were talking to those business types.'

Arjun was surprised by her boldness. He said, 'And why would you do that?'

'Well,' she said, 'you looked quite different from everyone else at the party, with your crumpled kurta-pyjama, so I was intrigued and wanted to find out who you were. I overheard the conversation you were having earlier, and I gathered that you are a communist – of the extreme leftist persuasion. I have never come across anyone who believed in the armed overthrow of the state, and it has made me wonder why anyone would put themselves into such danger.'

Arjun turned to look at Jyoti. Over a thin, almost emaciated body, Jyoti had a square face, large eyes set wide apart, and curly brown hair that fell in an untidy manner over her shoulders. Not an attractive woman by any stretch of the imagination, thought Arjun. And yet, there was something very appealing in the earnest and intense manner that she looked at him, so he felt compelled to answer her.

'If one allowed considerations of personal safety to decide one's goals in life, I don't think that most human beings who have achieved something of importance would have accomplished anything at all. Don't you think?' said Arjun. 'My decision to follow the path I am on is entirely based on my convictions of what is good for society at large, while being personally satisfying to me. People go to war and put their lives in danger because they believe in something. I don't think I am doing anything different.'

'True,' said Jyoti. 'But one can do a lot for society, and other people, without necessarily becoming an instrument of violence. I work with mentally retarded and disabled children, and you have no idea what a huge difference it makes to their lives to have the support of people who empathize with them.'

'Perhaps,' said Arjun. 'Interventions such as yours are very noble and may make a difference to a few lives, but if you want to improve the lives of the millions mired in poverty in India, radical social change is necessary, and if you read history, such change has generally come about through violent means. Anyhow, why do you have this issue with violence? Our birth into this world is a violent event. In fact, I believe that violence is an integral part of human existence.'

Jyoti shook her head. 'I don't agree,' she said. 'Unfortunately, I have to leave now, since I am getting a lift home from a friend. But I would really love to continue this conversation with you. I live in Jor Bagh, just opposite Lodhi Gardens. I am at home most evenings and weekends. So if you happen to be in the area, do drop in. Or if you have the time, come by our disabled children's home in Nizamuddin and see for yourself the value of the work that we do.' To be polite, Arjun smiled and said he would.

But he had no intention of doing so. Jyoti seemed like a nice and well-meaning person, but in his current state of conviction and confidence in his cause, she didn't really interest him. He would have never considered it possible that one day she would surface in his life again and even become a collaborator in the revolutionary movement.

It was now late and it would be difficult for Arjun to get back to the university area where he lived with his brother. So he asked Sundeep if he could spend the night in his apartment. Little did he, or the others, know of the momentous events taking place that night, which were going to affect his life and the history of India. That night the police raided Arjun's house, and had he been there he would have been arrested, perhaps tortured, and most certainly spent the next twenty-one months in prison.

ON THE NIGHT OF 25 June 1975, Fakhruddin Ali Ahmed, the weak and pliant President of India, also known as the 'rubber-stamp' President,[1] signed a proclamation at the behest of the prime minister, Mrs Indira Gandhi,[2] declaring a state of Emergency in the country. Under the Emergency law, the Constitution of India was effectively suspended, the democratic rights guaranteed by the Constitution were taken away, and Mrs Gandhi could rule by decree.

In the early hours of 26 June, most senior opposition leaders were arrested. Amongst them was Jayaprakash Narayan, the prominent Gandhian who had been leading the people's movement against the regime during the past few years. Thousands of activists across the political spectrum were arrested as well, with the number reaching more than 150,000 over the next few months. Many were beaten, some tortured and killed. The cases are too many to record. Arjun escaped this fate because he spent the night at Sundeep's apartment in south Delhi. That same night, a large police squad surrounded his brother's house at the university. The police entered the house and told all the family members to get out and stand in the driveway. The house was then searched thoroughly. They looked under the beds, in the cupboards, everywhere. Of course, Arjun was not to be found. He was not there. He was chatting with Sheila and Jyoti on Sundeep's terrace. The police then left, after threatening his brother with dire consequences if he did not reveal Arjun's whereabouts or his presence if he returned home.

Arjun in the meantime was quite unaware of all these momentous happenings. He left the apartment the next morning and took a bus to JNU. For several months now, he had been leading a political study circle of students interested in Marxism and current political developments in Indian society. The session was to be held in the evening, but he wanted to check if all the participants were back after the short holiday break. The study group sessions excited him and he looked forward to them. The discussions ranged from Stalinism and the failure of the Russian revolution, to Althusserian views of social consciousness, whether General Võ Nguyên Giáp's tactics were based on Sun Tzu's *The Art of War*, and of course, interpretations of current developments in Indian politics and society. The discussion and arguments in the study circle sharpened his mind and satisfied his intellectual cravings. And of course, he loved the hero worship of the students in the group! To them he was a true revolutionary, dedicating his life to the cause of the poor and downtrodden.

At the university he ran into Shekhar, who was horrified to see Arjun walking around casually in the campus.

He said, 'What the hell do you think you are doing, walking around in the open like this? Don't you know a state of Emergency has been declared? All opposition leaders and thousands of activists have been arrested. They are probably looking for you as well!'

Arjun was taken aback. The left-wing political group he was associated with had been discussing the increasingly authoritarian tendencies of the government and the likelihood of harsh measures being imposed on the opposition. But an open dictatorship being imposed overnight in this blatant and ruthless manner was unexpected. Nevertheless, in anticipation, structures had been put in place to meet this eventuality, and he was confident that these would enable him and other political activists to continue their anti-government crusade, albeit in more difficult circumstances. Through their organizational efforts, over the past two years, Arjun and his group had established a network of safe houses, or more appropriately 'safe huts', located in a number of slum areas in Delhi. The safest of the safe were in slums inhabited by the safai karamcharis or municipal workers. Here the government was not popular and the police would not venture readily.

It was mid-morning by now and an increased police presence, with armed policemen toting their guns menacingly, was now visible on all the major road crossings. Police cars were criss-crossing the city with their sirens screaming loudly. Arjun took the byways, lanes and the occasional bus ride to get across the Yamuna and into the slum area of Shahdara in East Delhi. In Seelampur, he met Ram Sewak. They decided that a meeting of the Delhi State Committee of their left-wing group should be called to discuss the situation and agree on a strategy going forward. Teenagers from the Harijan community were quickly mobilized and sent out as runners to other parts of Delhi to pass the message on to other activists.

In the next few days, demonstrations against the Emergency were organized by opposition parties and groups across the country. Most of these initial protests were led by the Hindu nationalist Rashtriya Swayamsewak Sangh (RSS), the Akali party of the Sikhs, and of course supporters of JP's Total Revolution movement. Their peaceful protests were suppressed brutally and thousands arrested. The leaders were already in jail. Seeing this, Arjun and his group decided that undertaking such public protests and getting arrested served no purpose. What was needed was to go underground and prepare for a long struggle against the dictatorial regime. Bringing about a socialist revolution would of course always be the fundamental goal of the group. But without any democratic rights, mobilization of the people would be that much more difficult. The revolution was therefore put on the back-burner, and it was decided that the strategy of the group now would be to work with like-minded political forces to bring about a restoration of democratic and constitutional rights.

With the new draconian laws and security measures in place, Delhi being the national capital had become an increasingly dangerous and difficult place to continue political activities. The group decided that a temporary retreat into the surrounding rural areas would be appropriate. One of the most important tactics of guerrilla warfare they had all read about, in the works of Sun Tzu, Mao Tse-Tung and others, was that when faced by an overwhelming enemy, it is best to retreat and conserve one's strength. The network of activists would therefore remain dormant for the moment, while Arjun and Ram Sewak would move base to Rajokri, a village in Mathura district in neighbouring UP. The village was mainly populated by Jat and Rajput small peasants. But it also had small enclaves of landless workers, and lower castes such as Harijans and Chamars. Rajokri was particularly suited as a refuge because there was already a group in that village that had participated in JP's movement, and several of them had become good friends with Arjun and Ram Sewak. It was agreed that in a month's time the situation would be reassessed to decide upon the next steps and the strategy and tactics for opposing the regime of Mrs Gandhi.

Angoori, Ram Sewak's wife, was in tears when she got to know that her husband was leaving. She had heard of all the atrocities committed on his family in Ballia and was afraid she was going to lose him forever.

'*Hai Ram*,' she said, weeping. 'We have only been married six months and you are already leaving me. What will become of me? Will I ever see you again?'

Ram Sewak, who liked using language from the Bollywood movies, said, 'Dil-o-jaan, I am just going away for a few days. I will be back before the next full moon shines on your pretty face.'

Angoori remained unconvinced. But the decision had been taken. The two travellers packed their things. Arjun had a few clothes and books, which he wrapped up in a small bundle. It would not be safe for Arjun and Ram Sewak to travel by bus to Mathura. All buses that crossed the border between Delhi and UP were being closely monitored by the police. They waited until dark and then set off on foot through the narrow lanes of the slums. By the early hours of the morning, they were across the Delhi state border in Ghaziabad. From there they boarded a bus for Mathura, and thence to the village near Vrindavan. For the last part of their journey, they hitched a ride on the bullock cart of a farmer who lived in the same village they were heading for.

At the village, they were met by Kanth, their friend and fellow activist. Kanth was sympathetic to ideas of socialism, but was an ardent supporter of JP's Total Revolution movement. His family were middle peasants owning about 6 acres of land, and belonged to the Jat community of western UP. In addition to cultivating his land, he was also a teacher at the local primary school. Arjun had met him at one of the meetings of opposition political parties held to organize the Delhi bandh in May 1974. Since then they had met several times, and Kanth would share Arjun's lodgings whenever he came to Delhi.

In the next few days and weeks, Arjun spent time reading the various books he had carried with him, by authors and thinkers like Tolstoy, Gogol and Lenin. He would bathe in the warm, gushing water of the tube well on Kanth's farm, and sit in the sugar-cane fields. He had a lot of time to think about his youth and childhood. As the son of a senior civil servant who had been to Doon School, St Stephen's College and Oxford University, the expectation would have been for him to join the Indian Administrative Service or perhaps a multinational bank in London. That he would soon be sitting on a charpai in Mathura district would not have crossed his wildest imagination while he was in Oxford. In the past few years, he had transitioned from a PhD student at Oxford to an underground political activist with a warrant for his arrest by the state. Is that what he wanted? Certainly, everything he had been doing in the past two years, since he had returned to India, had inexorably led in this direction. And now he was sitting in a sugar-cane field drinking doodh and dahi near Vrindavan, Lord Krishna's territory. Arjun was not religious, but as a child he had been exposed to the Bhagavad Gita, the great conversation in the Mahabharata between Krishna and the warrior king Arjuna. Strange, he thought, that he had the same name as the hero of the Mahabharata and was now in Vrindavan. Perhaps the gods were on his side and this was an omen for successful outcomes. But then Arjun, as a good Marxist, professed not to believe in gods or omens. Only time would tell.

7

Kites, Custard Apples and Mantras

ARJUN'S EARLY CHILDHOOD WAS typical of those of his class and background. His father had been a member of the Indian Civil Service (ICS). Prior to independence in 1947, this small group of elite civil servants had been at the core of the colonial system, managing the administrative structures of British India. Getting into the ICS cadre was extremely difficult. The entrance exam was highly competitive. One had to study an extensive curriculum and then spend time in England actually writing the exam. And then there was the interview to assess whether the candidate was fit to be a loyal officer of the British Empire. Joining the ICS had been a long and arduous journey for this young Brahmin boy from the religious district of Triplicane in Madras. But he had worked hard and persisted, and eventually joined the service in the early 1930s, returning to India to commence his career as a sub-divisional magistrate in one of the districts of the Madras Presidency.

Arjun's father was a true brown sahib. He dressed like an Englishman, had inculcated their values, and organized his life and that of his family based on these precepts and principles. As a civil servant, he believed in non-political allegiance to the government of the day. This of course meant total loyalty to His Majesty's government, which put him, and all the other Indian officers in the civil service, at odds with the nationalist movement. Nevertheless, he believed in fairness and justice, and did the best he could for the people in the district where he had administrative jurisdiction. He rose in the ranks steadily and was posted to the central government in New Delhi just before Independence. For these sterling services, Arjun senior was awarded the honour of Officer of the British Empire (OBE) by the Crown of England. The OBE was an embarrassment to Arjun senior, and the medallion had been hidden away, only discovered by the family in a musty old suitcase after his death.

Loyalty to the Crown resulted in vociferous demands from many in the nationalist movement for the dismissal of all the members of the ICS at the time of Independence. However, in spite of these demands, the new government of independent India decided that they needed all the expertise they could muster to speedily develop the country. In this endeavour, it was felt that the talents of such an elite group of administrators could not be wasted, and so they were absorbed into the new government. True to their values, Arjun's father and the other ICS officers switched their allegiance to the new government of independent India, and began serving it to the best of their abilities.

Arjun's mother, Naina, belonged to a feudal family from Hyderabad state. Her father, Raja Ramchander Rao, was the jagirdar of Narayanpet Samasthan or Little Kingdom of Narayanpet. Narayanpet had about eighty villages that provided the revenue to support the family. The raja had a passion for photography and became the official photographer in the court of the Nizam of Hyderabad. The family, however, fell into hard times when the raja died young and feudal disputes broke out over the lordship of the estates. Arjun's mother was then sent off to live with her elder sister, who was married to an officer in the British Army. Once she had finished her schooling and come of age, the family was very keen to get her married off. As a young woman of considerable beauty, she attracted many suitors from the feudal community in Hyderabad state. After several rounds of selection, the family zeroed in on the raja of Guntur. The raja was a man of substantial wealth, and the family felt that through an alliance with him, their fortunes could be revived.

An initial introductory meeting between the rich raja and the beautiful but impoverished young woman was set up. The raja arrived in all his finery, with a grand entourage and presents for all the girl's family members. The family was very pleased. The girl was now brought into the room. Her veil was lifted and the prospective couple was given their first person-to-person view of each other. Naina took one look at the raja and let out a horrified shriek. The raja was fat and ugly, with bushy eyebrows and greased back hair. There was no way she could see herself married to this man. She turned and ran out of the room. The raja was amused and not in the least offended by this behaviour. He liked what he had seen and was agreeable to proceeding with arrangements for the marriage.

Naina was distraught. She could not believe that her uncles were practically selling her off to this rich man in exchange for a large dowry. She begged and pleaded with her elder sister to call off the marriage. Eventually, her sister took pity on her and reached out into her network to find another boy. As it happened, Arjun's father had just returned from England after joining the ICS, and was also looking for a suitable bride. A small tea party was arranged to which the young man was invited.

From behind a curtain, Naina first got her glimpse of this shy, slim, white gabardine-suited boy from Madras. She loved the way he looked and immediately walked into the room to serve him tea, giving him her brightest smile and setting out to charm him. The rest was history.

Arjun was born in Delhi. His parents lived in New Delhi, the part of the city designed by the architect Sir Edwin Lutyens, where government functionaries and politicians had their residences. The suburb had spacious bungalows and broad tree-lined avenues. Their house was a stone's throw away from Birla House (renamed Gandhi Smriti in 1973), where Mahatma Gandhi lived. His mother was fond of walking over to Birla House from time to time, seeking darshan of the great man and hearing him speak. One of her favourite stories, and one that was always repeated with great solemnity, was that she had heard the shot that killed the great Mahatma. Arjun did not remember much of this. But one image from his early childhood that remained entrenched in his memory was that of a very benevolent-looking man with circular spectacles gazing at him, and then placing his warm hand on Arjun's head and saying a few words. In later years, Arjun would recall this memory and it would give him great comfort to think he had actually been blessed by the man who had brought independence to India.

IN THE MID 1950S, the family moved to Hyderabad. Arjun was about ten years old then. His father had been appointed to head the organization tasked with constructing the Nagarjuna Sagar dam. Once constructed, the dam would be the largest stone masonry dam in the world. Arjun was put into All Saints High School, an institution run by Sisters and Brothers of the Dominican Order. Initially he was very fearful of these stern-looking priests in their long robes. He had never been in an environment like this before. But soon he began to see that his teachers were not as scary as they looked. They were strict, but friendly and helpful.

Hyderabad was a truly magical period in Arjun's childhood. The family had moved into a house the size of a mansion in the posh, hilly suburb of Banjara Hills. In those days, the houses in this suburb were few and far between. They were mainly inhabited by families connected to the Nizam's feudal aristocracy. After finishing his homework, Arjun would wander out into the open hilly spaces strewn with huge boulders and rocky outcrops. Here he met many of the boys and girls of his age who lived in the vicinity. They became good friends: visiting each other's houses, exchanging storybooks and comics, and most of all, flying kites. Kite fighting was an obsession in Hyderabad. A string specially coated with fine glass, called manja, was affixed to the upper part of the twine that controlled a kite. Using this, one would swoop down their kite from high above on to that of a competitor and attempt to sever its thread. The ultimate goal of this battle was to earn the title of Nausherwan, or Killer of Nine Lions – kites in this case! However, neither Arjun nor any of his friends had ever managed to achieve this grand status. After a few skirmishes, the manja of even a skilful kite fighter would get worn out and the kite would be cut from the skies.

The competition amongst the kite flyers was so severe that there was a constant effort to find secret sources of manja supply. The gossip was that the best manja was available at a kite shop near Charminar, in the heart of the old city. However, in spite of several efforts to identify this source of supply, all the manja that Arjun bought from the kite shops in this area eventually failed to produce the desired results. He and his friend Mohammed, who lived nearby, therefore decided to make their own kite-cutting glass-coated thread. The project had to be carried out in great secrecy lest his parents found out and stopped it. The boys chose an empty outhouse on the compound for the operation. First, appropriate glass bottles were collected and crushed in an old stone mortar and pestle. This was then strained through a mesh to obtain a fine glass powder. The next step was to find the right gluing substance. They had been advised that the best glue to make manja was the syrup of a particularly thorny cactus plant found amongst the rocks in Banjara Hills. After several expeditions, the boys managed to collect enough of these plants for their project. With all the ingredients ready, the kite-flying twine was soaked in the cactus syrup and coated with the fine glass powder. This was then strung out to dry in the sun.

With the new manja Arjun felt he had the secret weapon which would render him a champion kite flyer. That Saturday, after school, he ran out to the field where all the boys gathered to fly their kites. Mohammed was there to help him. Up went his kite and gathered speed in the strong winds blowing that afternoon. Before he knew it, his kite had streamed sideways and severed the threads of the two kite flyers next to him. He and Mohammed shared a quick smile. Now they challenged a kite being flown by one of the older boys in the group. A quick skirmish and other boy's thread was severed as well. Two more victories followed soon after. A small crowd began to gather around Arjun and Mohammed. Defeating five kites was already a record in their group. Something unusual was happening. Then someone spotted a kite high up being flown from a rooftop far away. It was a bright red kite sparkling in the sunshine and dominating all the other kites in the sky. The crowd encouraged Arjun to let the wind take his kite even higher and fight this interloper. More thread was released and the kite flew higher. The red kite, not willing to allow a challenger, was upon him in an instant. The two kites clashed and swirled around furiously, their manjas cutting at each other. Suddenly, the crowd saw the red kite floating free. A loud cheer went up! But then Arjun's own kite thread lost its tension and went slack, and his kite floated off, free in the breeze. Still, this was an amazing feat. Arjun had cut six kites in succession, and this was cause for much excitement and celebration that afternoon.

While the title of Nausherwan was elusive, seethaphals or wild custard apples were plentiful in the hilly terrain. After their kite-flying battles, Arjun and his friends would search for bushes with ripe fruit amongst the rocks and ravines. They would split open the pods, enjoying the soft sweet flesh within and spitting out the black seeds like bullets. The next stop would be one of their respective houses, where they would be welcomed with mugs of tea and Indian sweets such as jalebis, gulab jamuns and ras malai. Sometimes Arjun would be so lost in all these activities that he would not notice evening had arrived and it had become dark outside. He would then be tracked down by his mother, taken home and given a scolding for being so irresponsible.

THEN THERE WAS HIS ayah or child-minder, Raziya bi. Raziya was frail and old, and looked uninteresting, but in fact had a very colourful past. She had worked as a maid in the household of one of the important Muslim nawabs in the court of the Nizam of Hyderabad. Her comfortable life as one of the minions in this royal court was, however, destroyed at the time of the partition of India in 1947. Her nawab had chosen to join those who supported the new state of Pakistan and had become an armed razakar, or rebel, in the area. There was fighting, and in the armed clashes the nawab was killed. Raziya escaped with her life and ran away to her village, only returning to Hyderabad many years later. She had come to work for Arjun's parents through some family connections, greatly reassured by the fact that Arjun's mother was herself the daughter of a pre-Independence feudal family. Such ties and loyalties were important to her.

Raziya bi had an amazing imagination and was a consummate storyteller. On evenings, after she had finished her household chores, she would sit with Arjun and enthral him with stories of Hatim Tai, the legendary Arab prince. Hatim Tai lived in the sixth century and is mentioned in the *Arabian Nights*. In the legend, a beautiful princess poses seven questions, and indicates that she will only marry a suitor who can solve these seven mysteries. Hatim Tai agrees to undertake this quest and a fantastic adventure full of sorcerers, dragons, other magical beings and untold wealth commences. Arjun had, of course, read the story of Sinbad and his seven voyages. But this was a completely different experience. It was one thing to read a book, but it was quite another to listen to the recitation of a story. Raziya bi would relate the episodes of Hatim Tai's adventures with modulation in her voice, changes in expression, and wild gestures. It made the characters and events so real that Arjun would be completely transfixed and feel as if he was part of the story itself. In his mind's eye he could see himself flying on a giant bird, collecting jewels on a beach, or moving around the desert on a camel with Hatim Tai, and experiencing all the incredible occurrences of the stories.

Sometimes Arjun would get impatient and ask Raziya bi questions. 'But bi, Hatim Tai was swallowed by the dragon. How did he not get eaten up and die?'

Raziya bi would patiently reply, 'Now, now, Baba, don't interrupt. Keep listening carefully and you will find out what happens next.'

Arjun could not remember when Raziya bi's storytelling began or ended. In later years it seemed to him that it had continued throughout the period he lived in Hyderabad, an unending story embedded in his memory forever.

WEEKENDS AND HOLIDAYS WERE the most memorable of all. Almost all of Arjun's mother's relatives lived in Hyderabad and he was constantly regaled by stories of the family's past. The stories not only fascinated him, but also made him feel connected to his roots. His brother, who was much older than him, was hardly ever at home. So he had grown up like an only child and felt the loneliness that goes with being one. But suddenly now there were several uncles and aunts, and a horde of cousins, many his own age. He found his uncles to be the most interesting people in this new-found family. His favourite was Rameshwar mama, who worked as a police officer in the city, but whose passion was performing magic. Rameshwar could do all the basic tricks that most magicians do. These included sleight of hand, correctly predicting cards picked by a person, reproducing a currency note that had been burned, producing rings and other jewellery out of the pockets of people, etc. All these and more would enthral Arjun and his cousins at their get-togethers. But the trick that proved to the kids that Rameshwar was a magician par excellence was his blindfolded driving event.

On their first 'magical experience' afternoon, Rameshwar first performed a series of standard tricks. He then informed the gathered relatives that he would drive a car blindfolded.

Nobody believed him, of course, until he actually started the preparations for this event. First, he had pats of dough placed over his eyes. Then a sack of cloth was put over his head, covering the face up to the neck. Finally, a large tin can, something like a small dustbin, was placed over all this. He then got into the car and asked the kids to jump in as well. All the parents present were horrified by this seemingly highly dangerous act, which could lead to a road accident and put their children in harm's way. They all protested vehemently. But the police officer reassured them that he was not going to put his own life in danger, and to prove that it was safe, he did a short and accident-free blindfolded spin on the long driveway that connected Arjun's house to the main road. With the kids, he then proceeded to take the car out on to the busy main road, and after navigating a few left and right turns, returned to the anxious parents standing by the house. The dustbin, sack, and bits of dough were then removed in full view of all to show that he had indeed been completely blindfolded. Nobody could explain how Rameshwar had pulled off this act. He never explained it to anyone, but always maintained that it was merely a trick. For Arjun, those were thrilling moments, sitting in the front seat and driving through Hyderabad traffic with a driver who could not see.

Arjun learned his family's history through his other uncle, Rajender mama. How much was fact and how much was fiction, Arjun never knew or cared. The stories were always gripping and fascinating. The early history of the family, according to Rajender, started with two brothers called Rai anna (brother) and Sai anna. They were adventurers who swept down into the Deccan with Mughal Emperor Aurangzeb's armies in the seventeenth century. There were many stories of how the two brothers participated in the successful year-long siege and eventual capture of the famous fort of Golconda in 1687. Apart from the battles they fought, a story of special interest was how they penetrated the fort through tunnels or other means, and forced open one of the gates so that the imperial forces could enter. For this valour, they were rewarded by Emperor Aurangzeb with a jagir in Hyderabad state. The estate was called Narayanpet Samasthan.

Rajender would recall his own childhood, when the whole family accompanied his father, Raja Ramchander Rao, to the rural estate. This would happen several times a year, particularly at harvest time or during the mango season. They would all travel in horse-driven carriages, with their servants and provisions, leaving Hyderabad in the early hours of the morning and arriving at the kothi at Narayanpet in the evening. Mango season was one of the most exciting times for the children. Mountains of the famous Rasam and Alampur mangoes of Hyderabad state would be brought to the kothi, and Rajender and the other kids would have mango-eating competitions, the winner being the one who could eat the most in a day. Under the feudal system in place in those days, the role of Rajender's father, the raja of Narayanpet, was primarily to collect taxes on behalf of the state of Hyderabad. He would ensure that all taxes and dues were collected as per the revenue records and these were then remitted to the treasury of the ruler of the state, the Nizam. The raja's agreed share of the tax revenue would be deducted first to finance his own expenses and administrative set-up.

Of course, this feudal structure did not care much about the conditions of the peasantry, who were taxed to maintain the extravagant lifestyles of the landlords and rulers of the kingdom. Narayanpet was in the Nalgonda district of Hyderabad, one of the poorest areas of the region. The high levels of taxation, combined with the poverty of the area, had led to much anger and discontent amongst the estate's peasantry. Rajender's father, the raja, was probably aware of these rumblings, but the family continued their sojourns in Narayanpet in complete bliss. However, all this came to an end in the mid 1940s with the intensification of the freedom movement in the area. The discontent amongst the peasantry was mobilized by the communists, leading to the Telengana rebellion. The peasants organized themselves, and through a violent struggle expelled all the landlords and agents of the feudal system from an area covering more than 4,000 villages. Millions of acres of land previously belonging to the various rajas who controlled the samasthans were then expropriated and redistributed amongst the poor. Nalgonda district was one of the hubs of this rebellion. After this rebellion, the visits of the family to Narayanpet ended.

Hearing all these stories, Arjun was keen to visit Narayanpet. His particular interest was to find out if the mango trees his uncle had so lovingly described were still there, and whether he could collect some tasty ripe mangoes and bring them back to Hyderabad. But his uncle warned him off.

'Baba, the area is infested by communists. If they find out you are a descendent of the raja's family, they may think you have come back to reclaim the family's lands and cut off your head,' he said.

This dire warning was enough to dissuade Arjun from trying to physically reconnect to his ancestry, or to look for mango trees in old estates and ancient forts where his ancestors may have fought. In any event, all this suddenly came to an end one day in 1959. His father returned one evening from the office, waving a letter in his hand.

'Congratulations, Arjun!' he said. 'You have been given admission to Doon School.'

Arjun did not understand what his father was trying to say. 'I go to All Saints High School, Daddy. I don't want to go to any Doon School,' he said.

'Don't be silly,' said his father. 'This is Doon School, the best school in India. It will be an exceptional experience, you will get a superb education, and you will become an independent and resourceful young man by the time you complete your schooling. Besides, the government has promoted me and given me a new job in Delhi. So we will all be moving to Delhi soon.'

Arjun started crying. He hated all this talk about moving to Delhi and Doon School. He loved Hyderabad and the magical life he was living there. He loved his school, his relatives, his uncles, Raziya bi, his kite-flying friends, and now it was all going to end.

And end it did soon. The family was moving to Delhi, and the term at Doon School would be beginning soon after. A big farewell lunch was organized by his uncles at the local Boat Club at which all the relatives and cousins were invited. There was much laughter and chatter about many of the interesting moments they had spent together in the last few years. Although he did not show it, Arjun was sick at heart because he knew that he was not going to see any of them again for a very long time.

THE SUMMER BEFORE ARJUN joined Doon School, he was bundled off to Rishikesh. The town is situated where the Ganga leaves the mountains and enters the plains. It was now a holy city, dotted with the ashrams of several Hindu groups and religious teachers. Arjun's eldest aunt, a widow and a person of strong religious inclination, lived in the Shivananda Ashram. She had renounced her family life and all her possessions, and had joined the ashram's ascetic order with the new name of Swami Ambikananda. Arjun's mother felt this was an opportune moment for him to become familiar with the Hindu religion and so he was sent off to spend a month there. At the age of eleven, therefore, Arjun was introduced to the many intricacies of Hinduism.

Life at the Shivananda Ashram was simple. The morning started early with breathing and yoga classes on a platform overlooking the Ganga. After breakfast, there would be lectures and classes on the content of the scriptures. Episodes from the Ramayana and the Mahabharata would be retold, with explanations of their real meaning and underlying messages. Students were made to recite sections from the Ramayana and memorize them. A lot of time was spent on the Gita, with its famous dialogue between Lord Krishna and Arjuna. Arjun loved to listen to the stories about Arjuna, the warrior king after whom he had been named. The gist of Krishna's teachings to Arjuna would be constantly repeated to the students. One must always do one's duty, irrespective of the reward or consequences. In that lay the path of righteousness.

Arjun's favourite mythological story was that relating to Ravana, the demon king. Arjun had been to several Dussehra celebrations where effigies of the ten-headed demon had been burned. The popular view was that Ravana was the epitome of evil. However, at the ashram he learned that Ravana was actually a scholar and a very learned person. His ten heads signified his mastery over the six shastras and four vedas, which taken together contained the wisdom of Hinduism. Ravana was also one of the greatest devotees of Lord Shiva. In his praise of Shiva, he had composed a poem in Sanskrit called the 'Shiva Tandava Stotram', which to this day is used as an invocation in temples where Shiva is worshipped. So Ravana had indeed done much that was evil, but he was also a great scholar who had made important contributions to Hinduism. Arjun was always spellbound by the manner in which Swami Jyotirmayananda, one of the ashram teachers, repeated the powerful-sounding words of the stotram. One could almost imagine the Lord Shiva furiously dancing the tandava, or dance of death, to the beat of these words.

> *Damad damadda mani nada vadda marvayam*
> *Chakaara chanda thandavam thano thuna Shiva! Shivum!*

Lord Shiva did the auspicious dance of tandava,
With the damaru making the sound Damat, Damat, Damat, Damat,
And may he shower prosperity on all of us.

Arjun's aunt spent a lot of time with him. She related to him story after story from the Hindu scriptures, and made him recite and learn important Hindu invocations. She said that the prayers would be his mantras in later life, give him peace in moments of difficulty and the strength to achieve his goals. Most important was the Mahamrityunjaya mantra, the mantra of immortality, from the Rig Veda.

> *Om trayambakam yajamahe sungandhim pushtivardhanam,*
> *Urvarukameva bandhanan mrityor moksheya mamritat.*

We worship Lord Shiva, the three-eyed,
Who emits the excellent fragrance that nourishes us all,

As a cucumber is released from its bondage to the stem,
So may we be freed from death to dwell in immortality.

Arjun had to repeat this 108 times a day using the beads of the new rudraksha mala that had been given to him by his aunt.

Evenings would be spent doing more chanting. Arjun's favourite was the Hanuman Chalisa, the invocation to the monkey god Hanuman, calling for his blessing and protection in life's journey. He particularly liked the shloka about ghosts and monsters staying away when they heard the name of Hanuman.

Bhooth pisach nikat nahi avay,
Mahavir jab naam sunawe.

All the ghosts and demons keep away,
Just with the mention of your name, O Mahaveer.

Another favourite line was the one that asked Hanuman to bestow eight supernatural powers and nine treasures to the devotee. These included the ability to obtain, acquire and have control over all things.

Ashta siddhi-nav nidhi ke dhata,
As var deen Janki mata.

You can grant to anyone the yogic power of the Eight Siddhis and Nine Nidhis,
A boon granted to you by Mother Janaki.

The Hanuman Chalisa had to be repeated seven times every day for maximum effect, and Arjun would do so religiously. He wanted all those magical powers!

Over the month, Arjun had memorized all these invocations and prayers. Many a time they would involuntarily repeat themselves in his mind, automatically, and without any effort or intention on his part. He may not have understood much about religion, or even been very religious, but by the time he left Rishikesh he had an armoury of mantras embedded in his subconscious.

8

Of Mountains and Men

THE TRAIN WAS PARKED on Platform 6, Old Delhi Railway Station. The morning rush hour had started and the station was bustling with life. The platforms were crowded with passengers looking for their trains, others checking if their names were on the carriage lists, railway conductors in their white uniforms looking important, and food vendors competing with each other for customers. Cries of 'Moom phalieee' (groundnuts) and 'Chai, garam chaieee' (Tea, hot tea) rent the air. Platform 6, however, presented a different spectacle. Here stood a special train, the Doon School Express, from Delhi to Dehradun, which was exclusively for students of the school. It was christened the Dosco Train. The train left Delhi in the morning and arrived in Dehradun the next morning. It was an institution in itself. The arrangement had been in existence for a long time and no one knew when it had actually started. Of course, there were a few teachers on the train to supervise the journey, but with so many boys on board, the control was minimal.

At Platform 6, there was none of the noise, pushing and shoving that is found in Indian railway platforms. Here the parents were all well dressed, in suits or similar formal attire, and moving around with an air of solemn dignity. The boys milled around excitedly in their blue-and-grey school uniforms, greetings friends they had not seen over the summer holidays. It was back to school now, with a new term and a new academic year beginning soon. On the platform, boys and their parents, with railway coolies in tow carrying their luggage, looked for the specific carriages they had been allotted. The carriages were organized in terms of seniority, with the older and more senior boys being placed in carriages closer to the rear of the train, and the juniors and newcomers being put in the front end near the engine. Arjun, being a newcomer, found that he was in the first carriage of the train, immediately behind the railway engine. His luggage was stored and his presence was noted by the teacher in charge.

The cabin he was in was a four-berth one, and Arjun found that the other three boys with whom he was to share the journey were already there. His parents continued to fuss over him, but Arjun was no longer interested in them. He was now more interested in the train journey, the possibility of inspecting the steam engine pulling the train, and interacting with the new boys in the carriage. His initial trepidation at leaving his parents and going off to a boarding school had all but dissipated. Sensing this, his father gave him a hug and said, 'Be good and enjoy school, son. It is going to be the best experience of your life.' His mother also hugged him and bade him a sorrowful goodbye. He was now on his own! Two of the other boys in his cabin were his own age. They were Sundeep and a Sikh boy wearing a turban named Harpal. The fourth, Kanwal, was a little younger than them and obviously missing his parents. He sat in the corner, sniffling away and looking out of the window.

The doors were closed, the guards made their last checks, the final whistle blew loudly, and then, in a cloud of steam and smoke, the train jerked to a start. They were off! A new journey had begun. A brand new world to explore. Arjun, Sundeep and Harpal settled into their cabin and soon took out the boxes of sweets and other goodies their parents had given them for the journey. They shared these amongst themselves, and also offered some to little Kanwal. But he was disconsolate and continued to sniffle in his corner. The other three, however, were enjoying themselves and had little empathy for the poor lonely boy. They were already becoming cruel little public-school boys. The train had now gathered speed and was bounding over the plains of northern India, heading for the foothills of the Himalayas where Doon School is situated.

Inside, the interaction between the new boys continued. Boys crowded into each other's cabins, particularly where sweets and chocolates were being offered, and Arjun got to know many newcomers like him, new friends who in time to come would become friends for life. At Saharanpur, the train stopped and moved onto a siding to let an oncoming train pass. The boys in the first carriage quickly got off and surrounded the engine. They begged the train driver to let them into the engine. Seeing all the enthusiastic faces, the good man finally agreed and Arjun got his chance to actually be in the driver's cabin of a steam locomotive. A huge coal fire roared away in the front, with bits of the flame flicking into the cabin itself. The control dials and pipes full of steam hissed away noisily, and then of course there was the wonderful steam whistle, which some of the boys got a chance to blow. But soon the signals changed, the boys were chased back into their carriages, and they were on the move again.

Night began to fall. The boys pulled out their sheets and pillows from their holdalls, and prepared for bed. Suddenly, the peace was disturbed by a group of seniors from one of the other carriages who barged into Arjun's cabin.

'Well, well,' said one of the seniors. 'Selfish little boys, all these toffees and sweets, and not sharing them with us. That's not verrry nice, is it?'

Arjun and his friends did not know how to respond; they were terrified. With trepidation they offered the intruders one of their boxes of mithai. This was quickly grabbed by the seniors and eaten in a flash. Then one of them turned his gaze onto Kanwal.

'Cute boy,' he said. 'I am sure we will be seeing a lot more of you once we get to school.' The others laughed and said, 'Yes, definitely, verrry cute!'

Arjun did not understand what all this meant, but this was his first exposure to the homosexual undertones of boarding-school life, something almost every boarder had to confront and deal with in their own way. After this, the seniors left. The train sped on through the night.

Morning came and with it the train began its winding journey through the Shivalik hills. The track wound through thick forests, crossing many streams and rivers. Soon they were in the Doon valley and could see the foothills of the mighty Himalayan ranges. Stations with strange names such as Tunwala, Doiwala and Raiwala went by, and then they were in Dehradun itself. Life at Doon School was about to begin.

Doon School was established in 1935. It was modelled on a British public school, but had a strong overlay and emphasis on Indian culture and traditions. 'Jana Gana Mana', the poem written by Rabindranath Tagore, became its School Song No. 1 in 1935, fifteen years before it was adopted as India's national anthem. The estate itself had previously been the Forest

Research Institute and was consequently bountifully endowed with evergreen and flowering trees and varieties of bushes. To the new boys there, it was like a magical kingdom full of trees to climb and secret hideouts to find for those enthusiastic enough to explore and experience what the estate had to offer.

Arjun fell into the routine of school quite happily. The school was organized into four residential houses, with about 100 students in each. Arjun was put into Tata House. The day started with a wake-up bell ringing at 5.30 a.m. Physical training was followed by breakfast, classes up to lunchtime, then sports and dinner. After dinner, there was time for homework and studies, which for some reason was called 'toye' time. Then lights out and bedtime by 9 p.m. All the teachers seemed to be considerate, sympathetic and humane. But the stars amongst them were definitely Gurdial Singh (Guru) who taught geography, Hari Dang who taught English, and Mr Holdsworth (Holdie), the Englishman who taught history. Guru and Hari were famous mountaineers who had been on Mount Everest. Hari had been on an unsuccessful summit party and had lost all his toes to frostbite. Because of the loss of these extremities, he never took off his socks. A total eccentric, Hari insisted that his name be pronounced 'Dung', not 'Dang'. Holdie's method of teaching was novel. He would ask one difficult question during every class and the first to answer it correctly would be rewarded with a juicy red apple, strategically placed on his desk for all to see. It was a mark of honour to win Holdie's red apple, and if you won it for a second time consecutively, you were considered the star pupil of the class!

Arjun had the greatest admiration for Hari Dang and Guru. Both teachers would regale their classes with stories of their trips in the Himalayas and mountaineering exploits. The class would listen spellbound to Hari's account of his attempt to climb the Everest when, unable to reach the peak, he had had to bivouac at about 27,000 feet. It was incredible that he had actually survived this night out in a snowstorm on the upper slopes of Mount Everest. That's when he had suffered frostbite and lost all his toes. Guru had stories of all the famous peaks he had attempted and climbed, including Trishul, Cho Oyu, Nanda Devi and others. More than a mountaineer, though, Guru was a true naturalist. He excited the imagination of the boys with his descriptions of the rivers and valleys, the flora and fauna of the mountainous region. To him it was as exciting to discover a rare flowering lily or blue gentian hidden in the rocks of some high valley as to climb a 20,000-feet peak. From him, Arjun acquired a love of the mountains, which was to stay with him for the rest of his life.

ARJUN'S YEARS AT SCHOOL rolled along. To him, one of the most exciting aspects of Doon School life was the mid-term break. At this time, the boys would be taken on a week-long trek into the high Himalayas. Initially, the groups would be accompanied by a teacher or two, but once they had reached their early teens, they would be allowed to organize their own group of friends and go off on a pre-defined route in the mountains. Arjun's first trip was to Dodi Tal, a lake in the Garhwal Himalayas. The group consisted of Ajay, Deepak, Sundeep and him. With packed rucksacks, the foursome boarded the morning bus to Rishikesh, the city of ashrams and yogis, on the banks of the Ganga. At Rishikesh, the Ganga makes its exit from the mountains into the plains. Here it looks like a heavenly river flowing down through the tresses of Lord Shiva – a beautiful, crystal-clear stream, sparkling in the sunshine. Further downstream at Haridwar, or even further at Varanasi, millions of people worship the Ganga as a holy river, but by then it has gathered all the filth of human habitation and sadly become just another of India's many polluted rivers.

From Rishikesh the boys boarded a bus to Uttarkashi. The road wound its way through the mountainous terrain, following the valley of the Ganga. It hugged the side of the mountain, with cliffs above and below, so narrow in places that two vehicles could not pass at the same time. One could only assume that the bus drivers who did these journeys on a daily basis knew every curve and danger spot to be able to navigate the road safely. The boys, however, were too occupied to be concerned about these perils. They were happily munching their biscuits and sweets, and enjoying the freedom of being away from school. Late in the evening, the boys arrived at Uttarkashi. From the bus stop, it was a short walk to the forest rest house, built some seventy or eighty years ago by British foresters. Out came the sleeping bags, and they were comfortably settled in for the night.

Early next morning the boys shouldered their rucksacks and the trek began. First, there was a short descent to the river. If they had continued along this track, they would have ended up at Gaumukh at the snout of the Gangotri glacier, where the Ganga is born. However, the route to Dodi Tal lay on the other side of the river. A fragile suspension bridge made from steel ropes and wooden planks had to be traversed. The bridge swayed ominously in the wind as the boys crossed it. From here, there was a steep ascent; up and up they went in the hot sun for several hours. Soon, however, they entered dense forests full of rhododendrons and pines. Being summer, the rhododendrons were all in flower – red, purple and pink splashed all across the mountainside. The air was full of the cries of monal pheasants and other exotic birds. The boys picked a nice spot amongst the pine needles and stopped for lunch. Unknown to them, Deepak had packed a bottle of liquor in his rucksack, and while the others were eating, he quickly slugged down a couple of big gulps of neat whisky! By the time they restarted their trek, Deepak was half-drunk and swaying around. So Arjun had to pull out the climbing rope he was carrying and tie all four of them in a line with Deepak in the middle. Everyone was very annoyed by this turn of events because it meant they all had to walk at a slow pace, bound together by the rope. But there was nothing to be done, as without this arrangement there was a serious danger of Deepak slipping off the pathway and rolling down the hillside.

In spite of the slow pace, the group arrived at Dodi Tal late in the afternoon. Dodi Tal is a small lake at around 10,000 feet, lying in a protected little hollow full of pine trees and surrounded by the high mountains. The waters of the lake were crystal clear and full of trout back then. On the banks of the lake was a small log cabin with bunk beds and a dining room. While the other began settling in, Ajay took out his fishing rod to try his luck at catching fish for dinner. He did not have to try very hard. The fish were so plentiful in this isolated lake that soon he had landed four good-sized brown trout. For his misbehaviour, Deepak was now ordered to gut, clean and cook the trout. Remarkably, he undertook this task without complaint, and an hour later, pan-fried fresh brown trout was served up for dinner. The boys ate hungrily, and then topped off the delicious meal with a tot of whisky each. A close eye was kept on Deepak to ensure he did not repeat his earlier antics of glugging down a quarter of a bottle at high speed. Before going to bed, the boys made sure that the front door of the cabin was securely bolted.

They had noticed some deep scratches on the outside of the front door, which had no doubt been made by some hungry bear trying to get in to the cabin, and they wanted to make sure no such intruder could get in that night.

Exhausted from their strenuous uphill trek, the boys were soon fast asleep. It was a moonless night. The darkness was impenetrable. Sometime after midnight, Ajay was woken up by a scratching and bumping sound on the front door. He quickly woke the others up. The scratching and bumping was getting louder and more frantic. The boys realized they were in trouble. There were bears outside trying to get in. The smell of the fried fish they cooked earlier and the remains left within the cabin was clearly attracting them, and they were desperate to get at it. The boys were terrified. It was like a nightmare. They were trapped in the cabin and had nothing to protect themselves with.

Then Deepak came up with an idea. He said, 'Let's pick up all our pots and pans and start clanging them together. Maybe the noise will scare them away.' The boys quickly picked up all the utensils in the cabin, stood next to the front door, and started hitting the pots and pans with whatever cutlery they could lay their hands on. The noise was deafening but it had the desired effect. The scratching on the door stopped and they could hear the bears grunting and running away. What a providential escape! The boys were relieved but remained fearful that the bears could return. To minimize the risk of a second attack, all the fish bones and other remains of the trout cooked earlier were collected and thrown out at a distance from the cabin. The rest of night passed uneventfully, and the boys even managed to get some sleep.

After the events of the night, they were all up very early the next morning. The valley and the lake looked so serene and peaceful that the terror they had experienced the night before was forgotten. Gentle mists hung over the lake. The trout were jumping high, trying to catch the night flies that still buzzed over the waters. Since this was the only day the boys had at Dodi Tal, they decided that rather than just lazing around the lake, they would climb up along the stream that entered the lake and see whether they could come out at some high point at the head of this small valley. It would be nice to get back to school and boast about being the Doscos to have reached the highest point ever in the mountains during a midterm break.

Not burdened by rucksacks now, the group raced up the slopes, crossing the stream several times, jumping over boulders, and skirting the large juniper bushes. Soon they had reached the ridge at the head of the valley. From here, the view was breathtaking. The grand Himalayan peaks were now close at hand. Just above them stood the icy upper slopes of Banderpunch, a 20,700-feet peak so near that one could almost touch it. Further behind were several other peaks including those of the Gangotri range. This was the first time that any in the group had been so close to the high Himalayas. They sat on the ridge for a while and enjoyed the beauty of the surroundings. But they had not forgotten their objective of climbing as high as possible on that day. On looking at the ridge, they found that there was indeed a high point a short distance away, after which the ridge fell away on all sides. Quick as a flash they raced to this point. On the survey map they were carrying, they found that this point was called Darwa Top, at a height of 13,600 feet. A small cairn of rocks was quickly built on the mini-peak, and then pictures were taken of a Dosco shirt flying on a stick. With this ascent, they were sure they would be the highest Doscos ever.

Over that weekend, they were back in school, and all the seniors who had been on treks exchanged notes. Alas, it was soon discovered that their good friends Alok, Gautam and his group, who had gone trekking in a valley nearer Gangotri, had reached a point at 13,750 feet, 150 feet higher than them! The disappointment was heavy. Still it had been a great experience, and the beginning of many more to come.

As Arjun grew older, the midterm treks graduated into full-fledged mountaineering expeditions. After his school-leaving exams, and during the summer break before joining university, he was invited by Hari Dang, the great Everester, to join a mountaineering expedition to a 21,700-feet peak called Jaonli in the central Himalayas. The peak had never been climbed before. This was to be a proper six-week expedition, led by Hari himself, with trained Sherpas accompanying them on the climb. Arjun's trekking friends Sundeep and Ajay would be there, as would the others like Alok and Gautam, with whom he had competed many times to do more arduous and higher climbs during the midterm breaks. Initially the expedition made good progress and it looked as if they would be successful in climbing the peak. However, in spite of several attempts the team could not get to the top. A safe route could not be found through the deep crevasses of the ice fall and icy ridges higher up on the mountain. Some of the expedition members were disappointed, but for Arjun, this did not matter. The experience of being in the high Himalayan valleys with friends was exhilarating and satisfying on its own.

More than the excitement of the expedition, however, in many ways the Jaonli trip signified the end of his childhood for him. Arjun had been appointed the quartermaster general by the expedition leader, Hari Dang. In this capacity, he was expected to hand out rations to the cook every morning for the meals to be made. On this particular day, Arjun had wandered down to one of the tea shops on the road head, where the team was waiting for transport to take them back to Dehradun. He discovered that the owner was frying jalebis. What a treat, he thought, after six weeks in the mountains. Arjun sat at the tea stall while they were being fried and then spent the next hour or so slowly savouring the hot jalebis and milk. He completely forgot about the food needs of the other team members. Having catered to his sweet tooth, he returned to the camp, still failing to remember that he was to hand out rations to the cook. Hari was in a fury when he found out about this delinquent behaviour.

'You idiot! You incompetent ass!' shouted Hari angrily. He rushed over to where Arjun was sitting with a replete look on his face and swept him off the chair with a blow from his gun butt. Arjun was utterly stunned and speechless. He was indignant that the teacher he had adored throughout his school days had abused him and knocked him to the ground in this ignominious manner, as if he were a small child. But he did not see himself as a child any more. He had finished with school and was going to be a student at Delhi University soon. Sure, he had made a mistake, but he felt he was now a grown man, and expected to be treated as one. The aura of being a cocooned schoolboy had been shattered forever. Doon School or no Doon School, he was not willing to be treated in this manner by anyone. Doon School had taught him to become a resourceful and self-reliant young man. The time had now come to move on.

ARJUN FOUND THE HOMOSEXUALITY prevalent amongst certain circles in the school incomprehensible. He did not find young boys to be sexually attractive and could not understand why some seniors were so inclined and preyed on the juniors. His adolescent mind could not grasp the fact that such abuse was probably more a reflection of the emotional problems of troubled young men growing up together, in a closed environment, without any exposure to the opposite sex. Thus, their behaviour was probably a result of adolescent hormones rushing through their semi-adult veins without any outlet rather than anything else. Nevertheless, Doscos were ridiculed as 'homos' by most other elite public schoolboys, and they hated this label. Unfortunately, the school management and teachers at that time, seemed to be quite unconcerned about these goings on, and pretended that the issue did not exist. The problem was compounded by the fact that senior students had undue power over the youngsters. The school had a system of self-policing whereby some seniors were appointed as prefects or monitors to maintain general discipline. This system gave the boys appointed to such positions a great deal of authority over their fellow students. As a result, some of those appointed misused this authority to harass those younger than themselves with unwanted physical advances or other abusive behaviour.

Luckily for Arjun, he was not considered a cute or enticing boy. Therefore, for the most part, he went about his usual school activities quite peacefully without coming to the attention of some of the more notorious prefects like Vishwas, whose sexual predilections were known to all. In the few times Arjun was accosted, though, he had developed stratagems to escape this unwanted attention. If called by a senior to go sit next to him on a bed, he would say, 'Have just been given a task by Suman [another prefect], will be back in a minute.' And then he would run off. Or if he were grabbed in some lonely spot, he would say, 'I say, can't you see there are too many people watching around here,' and then quickly escape while the senior was checking to see if anyone else was near them. What the fate of those considered cute or 'hot' was, Arjun never fully knew. There was poor little Kanwal, the fourth passenger in the railway compartment during Arjun's first journey to the school. He was harassed all the time. And then there were others like Mirchi – the hot chilli – who was the 'hit' of Arjun's second year in school. Perhaps they had their own stories and had developed their own ways of evading the advances of their admirers. No one ever knew because it was taboo to talk about it, and eventually they all left school as grown-ups, leaving all these stories, events and mishaps behind.

In all his years in school, Arjun only let his guard down once, and was severely punished for this little lapse. It was late in the evening one day, when he was returning to his room from chess practice. As it was the middle of summer, some of the prefects had been allowed to move their beds from the shared bedrooms into the outer corridors. The notorious Vishwas was sitting with Mirchi on a bed in one of the corridors. They were talking in low tones. As he walked past, Arjun glanced at them and sniggered. Vishwas heard the snigger and looked up at him with a face contorted in rage.

'You, boy, come here!' he screamed in anger. Arjun stepped away from Vishwas fearfully. In the meantime, Mirchi had disappeared quietly from the scene.

'I will teach you to be disrespectful. Bend over,' roared the prefect.

Arjun knew he was now going to be spanked with a cricket bat. A painful punishment from which there seemed to be no escape now. Just then, another group of seniors returning from evening extra-curricular activities passed by. Suman, one of the other prefects, was with them. Seeing the scene, he asked Vishwas what was going on. Vishwas was of course too embarrassed to relate what had actually happened.

'Rude boy, just teaching him a lesson,' he said dismissively.

'Ah, come on,' said one of the others. 'Just let him go.'

At this Arjun quickly jumped up from his bent-over position and ran off. What a providential escape, he thought. But it taught him a lesson for the rest of his days in school, and he certainly made an effort to keep out of the way of dangerous seniors like Vishwas.

DOON SCHOOL WAS ALSO where Arjun came across Sanjay Gandhi for the first time. This was the early 1960s, and Sanjay's mother, Mrs Indira Gandhi, was not yet Prime Minister of India. She had just entered the political fray and was president of the Congress Party. Sanjay and Arjun were in the same year and same class. But while Arjun, like most other students, was intent on doing his best at studies and playing an active role in school life, Sanjay had no such interests. His behaviour was frivolous, erratic and at times dangerous. He had no respect at all for authority. In class, it was risky sitting next to him. Many a time in maths class he had grabbed Arjun's sharpened pencil and stubbed it so that the pencil's point had broken. He was known to quietly hide instruments from the mathematical box of the student sitting next to him, and would become aggressive when questioned about this. In one such incident, when accused by a fellow student, he whipped out the steel-tipped geometry compass he had hidden and stabbed it into his neighbour's table, missing the student's hand by a fraction. On another occasion, to cause trouble for the entire class, he put stink bombs under the class teacher's chair. This resulted in the whole class being suspended and being sent to the headmaster. Since, in good public-school tradition, no one owned up to this crime, the whole class was punished for his misbehaviour.

Arjun thanked his lucky stars he was not in the same residential house as Sanjay, and avoided him as much as he could. However, in spite of this he inadvertently once fell under the fellow's sway. It was Saturday night. Each week this was 'entertainment night' at school, which meant that an old or classic movie would be screened. The boys always longed to go to one of the theatres in town, where the latest movies were showing. This was of course not possible since all students had to stay within the school boundaries, and town, though only a stone's throw away across a dry riverbed, was considered out of bounds. Then one day the boys heard that Alfred Hitchcock's famous thriller *Psycho* had come to town. This was a must-see, worth the risk of breaking bounds, hopefully without getting caught.

The movie show was at 9 p.m. Arjun and two of his friends got to the boundary wall at the bottom end of the school overlooking the riverbed. None of the night guards could be seen. They were about to jump the wall when there was a rustling in the bushes next to them. Before they could retreat from the wall, they found Sanjay and a friend beside them. They too were planning to break bounds and go to the movie. However, they seemed to have a devil-may-care attitude and were being very noisy and clumsy in their efforts to get over the wall. Arjun was scared. If the night guards caught them, they would be severely punished by the headmaster. He turned to Sanjay and said, 'Can you tone down the racket and move more silently?'

Sanjay was angry at being reprimanded. He walked up to Arjun, slapped him hard across the face, and said, 'Now you shut up and do as you are told. I know what I am doing. Follow me and let's jump the wall.'

Arjun was so shocked by this aggressive behaviour that he meekly followed Sanjay over the wall, over the riverbed, and to the movies. There was no further incident and after the movie, the group slipped back into school. Then, as a parting shot, Sanjay said to the others, 'See, we had fun. You just have to listen to me and all will be well.'

That was the last Arjun saw of Sanjay until they met again in early 1975, before the imposition of the state of Emergency in June that year. The following term Sanjay did not return to school. There were many stories of his lack of academic performance, disrespect and the chaos and trouble he had caused. The story goes that Jack Martyn, the headmaster, had visited his mother, Mrs Gandhi, and told her that Sanjay should be withdrawn from the school. As a consequence, Sanjay dropped out and did not come back to Doon School the following term. But for Arjun, the slap had left a lasting impression. Sanjay was a bully and a terror: his traits would haunt the Indian political system in the years to come.[3]

9

Ram Sewak

WHILE ARJUN WAS GROWING up as the privileged son of a senior government official, a long way away in a small village in district Ballia of Uttar Pradesh, another little boy was enduring a much more difficult childhood. Ballia is in the eastern part of UP, bordering the state of Bihar, and one of the poorest regions of the country. The boy's name was Ram Sewak. His father belonged to the Bhangi or 'untouchable' caste. Mahatma Gandhi had tried to remove the stigma associated with this group in the Hindu caste system by renaming them Harijans or 'people of God'. However, given the rigidity of the caste system, with its deep-seated and age-old traditions, the discrimination continued. Ram Sewak was born in independent India. But for his caste, independence had brought no salvation. His community continued to live in their own basti, isolated from the rest of the village, with their own separate open well for water supply, and strict codes of conduct which prevented them from entering those parts of the village inhabited by the higher castes unless it was for work or some other acceptable purpose.

The Harijan community in the village were the poorest of the poor. None of them owned any land. Most of them worked as seasonal labour for the higher castes, with only a few privileged families amongst them graduating into becoming sharecroppers for the bigger Rajput landlords. A sharecropper was allowed to cultivate the land of a landlord, and in return for this would share his produce with the landowner.

Ram Sewak's father, Bhagwan Din, was one of the privileged Harijans. He was a sharecropper for Thakur Dharam Singh, the largest landowner in the village. He had achieved this position through his participation in the freedom struggle against British rule in India. As a young man, he had been inspired by the courage and leadership of Mahatma Gandhi, and had attended meetings of the Congress Party in Ballia town, eventually joining the party in the early 1940s. His participation in the freedom movement reached its culmination in 1942, when the Quit India movement was launched. Initially, non-violent demonstrations were held all over Ballia district against British rule. However, these acts of passive resistance were met with great brutality from the British administrators in Ballia, with merciless beatings, imprisonment and the torture of protestors. This angered the people of Ballia so much that on 19 August 1942 a huge crowd mustered whatever weapons it could get and attacked the district administration headquarters. After a short battle, the British gave up the fight and quickly escaped. Ballia was declared 'independent' by the victorious leaders of the movement. Bhagwan Din was very much part of this event. The group he was with attacked the district jail, freed all the prisoners, and hoisted the national flag. His role in the struggle was therefore well known to the Congress leaders.

The 'independence' of Ballia was short-lived. The British brought in the army and the revolt was suppressed with ferocity:

many of the nationalist leaders were killed and hundreds imprisoned. As a result of these events, Ballia became part of the history of the freedom struggle, and the region came to be known as 'Baaghi Ballia' – 'Revolutionary Ballia'. For the moment, however, Bhagwan Din quietly escaped back to his village. Thakur Dharam Singh was also part of the Congress Party. Of course, as a large landlord, with land, property and other interests to protect, he never openly participated in any anti-British activities. Instead, he quietly gave donations to the Congress Party. Nevertheless, due to his association with the party, he got to know about Bhagwan Din's role in the 1942 movement. Consequently, he had a soft spot for him and had made him a sharecropper on his land. However, a Bhangi was still a Bhangi, and freedom fighter or not, within the village, the rules of the caste system still prevailed. In the village, Thakur Dharam Singh remained the powerful high-caste overlord, while Bhagwan Din continued to be an 'untouchable' menial.

THE SECOND WORLD WAR came to a close in 1945 and soon after that India became independent. There was much celebration in 'revolutionary' Ballia. The sacrifices of all those men and women who fought against the British had not gone in vain. But the economic and social conditions in the district remained dire. Eastern UP was an area subjected to repeated droughts, and Bhagwan Din and his family continued to eke out a desperate existence. The dire situation in the area led to many men from the landless and lower castes leaving the district in search of employment in towns and cities far away.

Bhagwan Din, however, continued to live and work in the village. A few years after Ram Sewak was born, Bhagwan Din and his wife had a baby girl. She was named Chandi. With a family of six, including his old parents, to feed, Bhagwan Din was now totally dependent on Thakur Dharam Singh and the small patch of land that had been given to him to cultivate. Politicians would come to the village and there was much talk of Five Year Plans and how the government was going to bring prosperity to the rural areas. In practice, however, the only new development in the village was the construction of a primary school. The school was inaugurated with great fanfare, and the opening ceremony graced by the local MP. There was great excitement amongst the poor, landless and lower castes in the village. Their children were finally going to get access to education. They would not remain illiterate like their parents. However, on the first day of school, when all the primary school-age children of the village gathered to get admission, there was consternation amongst the Brahmins, Rajputs and other upper castes. It was out of the question for their children to mix with the untouchables and other lower castes in the school premises. The schoolteacher was summoned by the Panchayat and ordered to exclude the lower-caste children from admission to the school. The teacher, being an educated person from the nearby town, refused to do this and immediately suspended all operations of the school.

Over the next month, there was much wrangling on how to resolve this issue. The school remained closed. The local village committee was dominated by the upper castes and refused to budge on its position. Eventually, Bhagwan Din and other low-caste community leaders took this matter up with the leaders of the Congress Party in Ballia town. Their intervention finally yielded some results. It was agreed that the school could admit lower-caste children, but they would have to sit as a separate group, in the rear of each classroom, and not mingle with the other children. To Bhagwan Din and his fellow community leaders, this was a major victory. At least now their children would get an education. It was thus that Ram Sewak got to attend school, and learned how to read and write. His daily routine consisted of attending school in the morning, and then spending the afternoons either with his father in the fields, or playing with his little sister in the basti. Sometimes he and a group of other children from his community would go to the nearby waterhole. There they would swim or try and ride on the water buffaloes that wallowed in the muddy waters.

THE YEARS ROLLED BY. Ram Sewak's grandparents passed away. Chandi grew up to be a pretty girl. It was now 1967, and Ram Sewak was twenty years old. Very little had changed in the village, and Ram Sewak, with his primary-school education, had a yearning to improve his situation in life. There was nothing for him in the village, and so he begged his father to speak to his old acquaintances in the Congress Party in Ballia town and get him a job there. Many of those with whom Bhagwan Din had participated in the 1942 uprising were senior members of the administration there now. Through their good offices, Ram Sewak got a job as a safai karamchari in the municipality of Ballia. His job was to collect all the rubbish and filth in the streets of the town and keep the public toilets clean. After all, he was a Bhangi and this was a natural job for him. Ram Sewak didn't mind the menial nature of his work. He had a job, he was out of the village, and he was now a town dweller. Unlike in the village, he was free to interact with people of other castes and develop social relationships. In particular, he loved the daily opportunity to wander into the premises of the municipality office and read the local and national newspapers. In this way, he developed his knowledge and understanding of the world around him and the events occurring in the nation.

The year 1967 was a momentous one. The economy had been performing poorly for the past decade, with poverty rising to alarming levels. Mrs Indira Gandhi had won the leadership contest in the Congress Party in 1966 and had become prime minister. But the general elections in this year were the first time she had to face the electorate. The results of the election were a shock for the Congress. For the first time since Independence in 1947, the Congress Party fared badly. Although it had been voted back to power at the national level, this time around it only had a slim majority in Parliament. At the state level, the Congress lost its majority in eight of the sixteen states, and non-Congress governments were formed in these eight states, including in neighbouring Bihar. In West Bengal, a leftist government took power in which the CPI (M) had a significant role. The winds of change were blowing through India.

Then in May 1967, an event occurred that was to have a profound effect on class relations in rural areas, and on the social consciousness of the younger generation all over the country. After the leftist victory in West Bengal, expectations were high that the socioeconomic injustices in the state, particularly relating to the skewed distribution of land, would be addressed. However, when this did not seem to be forthcoming through normal administrative and legal channels, a group of peasants led by the local Communist Party took matters into their own hands in a small village called Naxalbari. There was an armed uprising resulting in the state administration being chased away. The local people then declared the area to be a self-governing commune; land was confiscated from the landlords and redistributed to the peasantry. The uprising was soon suppressed by the police, but a spark had been lit.

Naxalbari marked the beginning of greater militancy on the part of tribals, the landless and the poor peasantry in independent India. Landlordism and a highly unequal distribution of land had been inherited from the colonial times, but in the two decades of Independence successive governments had done very little about this. The communist group that had led the Naxalbari uprising now split away from its parent organization and formed the Communist Party of India (Marxist–Leninist). It now advocated armed insurrection against the state. This call was heeded by thousands of youths who had seen little economic progress in their lives, including many from the educated and intellectual elite who believed that the solution to India's poverty lay in following the revolutionary path laid out by Mao Tse-Tung in China. Inspired by these ideas, students and intellectuals now started migrating from the cities to the rural areas, and organizing the peasantry against the landlords and other propertied classes. Widespread clashes began occurring between the militants, now called 'Naxalites', the peasants that they had mobilized, and the upper classes supported by the forces of the state.

BALLIA DISTRICT COULD NOT be immune to all these happenings. Historically, in eastern UP, as in neighbouring Bihar, the upper-caste Bhumihars owned most of the land, employing other sections of the peasantry as tenants, sharecroppers or just wage-earning labourers. To protect their properties and enforce their dominant position in society, many of the land-owning castes had formed private armies called senas. The senas included the Ranvir sena of the Thakurs; the Savarna sena of the Bhumihars; and the Kunwar sena of the Rajputs, amongst others.[4] These senas were ruthless enforcers, beating, mutilating, raping and even killing those that dared to commit any transgressions against the authority of the landlords.[5] Thakur Dharam Singh and his caste allies in Ballia also had such an armed sena. It was led by Ranbir Singh, his eldest son. When clashes started occurring between the communist militants and the landlords in neighbouring Bihar, Dharam Singh and the other landlords in his village decided they should consolidate the grip on their own lands by expelling all the lower-caste tenants who had been cultivating these lands. Bhagwan Din and all the other tenant farmers were summarily kicked off their plots and told not to return. Tensions ran high in the village. There were even rumours that a dalam, or squad of armed Naxalites, had been seen in the forests near the village.

Bhagwan Din could not believe that social relations with the landlords had deteriorated to such an extent in their village. He was concerned that without access to the little plot of land he had been cultivating for years, he would not be able to feed his family. For the past two years his daughter Chandi had also been allowed into the Thakur's haveli, where she would sweep and clean the premises. For this she was receiving a tiny wage, but nevertheless it contributed to the upkeep of the family. Bhagwan Din hoped that his long years of association with the Congress Party, and the fact that Dharam Singh himself was a member of this party, would carry some weight and enable some compromise to be reached. Gathering his courage, he went over to the haveli to request an audience with the Thakur. The outer door to the compound was opened by one of the louts who belonged to the Thakur's sena.

'What do you want?' said the man. Bhagwan Din explained his mission. The man glared at him and then said, 'Come inside.'

Inside the haveli compound the landlord's son, Ranbir Singh, and several of his minions were having their evening meal and drinking tharra, the local alcoholic brew.

'So, the leader of the Bhangis has come to visit us,' he sneered.

Bhagwan Din spoke of his mission with the greatest humility. He indicated that he and the other lower castes in the village had the utmost respect for the Thakur and his family, they were bound by the age-old traditions, they did not support the Naxalite violence occurring in nearby districts, and they wanted the landlords to reconsider their decision to evict all the tenants from their lands.

Ranbir Singh was half-drunk. Bhagwan Din's words drove him into a fury. He said, 'How dare you, an achoot, come into my house and tell me what to do? We know what your plot is. With the support of those thugs from Naxalbari, you want to forcibly grab all our lands. Well, that's not going to happen. We have our own sena as well. At the slightest sign of rebellion, we will string you all up the nearest tree. Now get out of here and don't come back.'

Having delivered his threat, Ranbir and the louts continued to drink. Bhagwan Din was crestfallen. He returned to the Bhangi part of the village and visited some of the other ex-tenants to give them the bad news. By the time he got home, it was late. Chandi had not yet returned home. He was not concerned as she sometimes visited her friends in the basti and stayed on for a while. However, as the night wore on, he became increasingly worried because she had not arrived yet. But there was little he could do. Unbeknownst to him, Ranbir Singh and his louts had imprisoned Chandi that night, and gang-raped her.

Morning came, and there was still no sign of Chandi. The elders organized a search party to look for her in the village. They even entered the upper-caste areas of the village to enquire if anyone had seen her. On passing Dharam Singh's haveli, they came across one of the sena members. He just guffawed and said, 'Perhaps the Naxalites have kidnapped her.' Bhagwan Din and his wife were at a complete loss. Where could Chandi be? Unable to find her, the next day Bhagwan Din went over to the nearby police post to seek their assistance. The officer-in-charge was unsympathetic. Lower-caste girls disappeared all the time, he said. Sometimes they ran off with boyfriends, at other times they escaped to the towns and cities to look for a better life. However, since he knew that Bhagwan Din was a member of the Congress Party, he agreed to send a constable to assist in the search for the girl. By the time they got back to the village though, the shocking news had already spread. Chandi was dead. She had been found hanging from a tree near the waterhole where the buffaloes swam.

Bhagwan Din was beside himself with grief and anger. He knew this was the landlord's punishment for his boldness in asking that the small tenants in the village be given back their land. It was also a message to all the lower castes that any effort to challenge the landlord's authority would be severely punished. Chandi had last been seen in Dharam Singh's haveli. But the landlord, his son and his minions denied having seen her after she had completed her daily work and left the house. However, Bhagwan Din knew what had happened. He went back to the police station to make a complaint.

This time around, the officer in charge was even more uncooperative. He said, 'Now you listen to me. Chandi was found hanging on a tree. She may have committed suicide. There was no indication of foul play. There was even less indication that the landlord's son was in any way involved.'

The police officer also warned Bhagwan Din that he was treading on dangerous ground making accusations against the landlord's family. At the end of the interview the officer told Bhagwan Din that while he would make some enquiries into this case, he would not allow him to file a police report in which the names of Dharam Singh or any of his family members was given, and that was final. Bhagwan Din was now left to nurse his inconsolable grief.

Ram Sewak was informed about his sister's death the next day. Back in the basti there was outrage and much anger. Ram Sewak and his friends knew that Ranbir Singh was responsible for murdering his sister. But the police were on the landlord's side, and so he and his family would never get any justice. There was consensus amongst the Bhangis that the landlord should not be allowed to get away with such a heinous act. He must be punished. Some of the youths even suggested that they should contact the Naxalites who were active nearby. The matter was left at that, and after the cremation, Ram Sewak went back to Ballia. But of course, the Naxalites themselves operating in the area had heard about this atrocity, and soon one of their activists contacted Ram Sewak to offer their support. This was the first time that Ram Sewak had had contact with the Naxalites. He was very apprehensive. But the activist, a student from Calcutta University who had given up his studies to join this movement, was very persuasive. The activist gave his name as Bose. Ram Sewak was certain that this was a pseudonym and not his real name.

During the next month, Ram Sewak and Bose met several times. Ram Sewak was given literature on Marxism. Discussions were held about the progress made by China after the communist revolution, and why poverty and exploitation in India could not be eliminated without a fundamental change in its political structure. Bose also explained to Ram Sewak that the current social structure in the rural areas had been inherited from the feudal and colonial times, and that since the present government was dominated by the same propertied classes who controlled the land and other resources, no real change could occur. The need of the hour was to mobilize the poor for revolutionary change, and for this purpose he should spend more time in his village organizing those of his class. Ram Sewak was inspired by these ideas and began spending more time in his village. Soon he had organized several cells amongst the lower caste and unemployed youths in his basti. They were now ready to support the Naxalite squads operating in neighbouring districts.

It was about two months since Chandi had been raped and murdered. For the past several weeks, Ram Sewak's cells had been unobtrusively observing the movements of Dharam Singh, his son and the eight or nine Thakur sena members who hung around the haveli. They found that on Sundays, Ranbir and his louts drank particularly heavily and then passed out or fell asleep. Ram Sewak passed on this information to his Naxalite contact. The following Sunday a squad of armed Naxalites attacked Dharam Singh's haveli. The sena goons, drunk and outnumbered, offered no resistance. The squad entered the house and brought out Dharam Singh and his son Ranbir. They were tied up and taken to the village square. The Naxalites then gathered as many villagers as they could find and summarily executed the landlord and his son. Their dead bodies were then left for all to see. The squad disappeared into the night.

The news of the landlord killings in Ballia spread like wildfire. The politicians screamed at the top of their voices: the Naxalite scourge had now spread to UP, the government was not providing protection to respected members of the community, law and order had broken down, no arrests had been made. The landlords in the area, for their part, immediately called their own conclave. This challenge to their authority could not be tolerated. The lower castes had to be taught a lasting lesson. They knew that the origins of the problem lay in Ram Sewak's basti. The senas were mobilized for an attack. Meanwhile, having observed the revenge taken by the landlords once, and fearful of further retaliation, Ram Sewak escorted his parents out of the village and took them to Ballia town to stay with him. He also advised his fellow caste members who had formed Naxalite cells to temporarily stay away from the village. The attack of the senas on the basti was brutal. Armed thugs numbering more than 100 attacked the area and set fire to all the huts. Many women and children were burned alive. The government shed crocodile tears about this atrocity, but none of the perpetrators was arrested. The attack served to intensify the class conflict in the area. Most of the lower-caste youth became active members of the Naxalites, with many of them joining the squads as armed militants.

Ram Sewak knew this was the end of the line for him in Ballia district. His home had been burned down and there could be further reprisals against his parents at any time. It was time to leave. Bhagwan Din had a cousin who had left the village a long time ago and was now working in Delhi. They decided that was where they needed to go. So in early 1969 Ram Sewak arrived in Delhi. Based on his experience in the municipality of Ballia, he got a job as a sweeper in the Delhi administration. His uncle helped the family to find a hut in the vast Harijan basti of Seelampur, in Shahdara, east Delhi.

10

Jyoti

JYOTI WAS THE ULTIMATE spectator. Everyday life was like an unending film script, with her as the lone moviegoer sitting in a cinema hall, watching the events flash by. The events and occurrences, happiness and sorrow, injustice and horror, would all unfold before her, and she could – and would – emotionally react to it all; but because of her physical disabilities, she was never in a position to influence anything.

Jyoti was born in Baroda to a Gujarati Brahmin family. Her father was a prominent businessman involved in the import and distribution of synthetic textiles. The young in the 1960s, a new post-Independence generation influenced by Western fashion, were moving away from the traditional khadi and cotton clothing in the market, and demanding clothes made from polyester, terylene, viscose, nylon, and other shiny synthetic fabrics. Her father had made a small fortune trading in these items.

In spite of their wealth, the family continued to live in Alkapuri, the neighbourhood of Baroda they had always lived in.

The houses were small, allowing for little privacy, with many uncles, aunts and people of the same caste living in the area. There were some non-Gujarati immigrants, but these were few and far between. Each house had its own private mandir, with a plethora of pictures and statues of Hindu gods and goddesses, to whom prayers were offered every morning and evening. No activity could commence without the appropriate offerings being made to the gods. To do otherwise would be most inauspicious and invite bad luck. Jyoti's mother was uneducated, from one of the villages in Surat district, and had been married off in an arranged marriage at the age of fourteen. She managed the household efficiently and strictly according to the prevailing social customs of their Brahmin community. To her, the roles of men and women in society were well defined and cast in iron. She was against all forms of modernism, and considered the idea that men and women are equal to be immoral.

Jyoti was an only child. If her mother had had her way, she would not have been sent to school. However, her father, a follower of the Mahatma's teachings, insisted that the education of the girl child was important. So she was sent to school, but not allowed to study or read any books at home beyond what was required as homework from school. In reaction to these restrictions, Jyoti became an avid reader. She would devour books secretly. Books would be hidden under the table at lunch and dinner; she would take a book with her during the weekly visit to the temple, and even on social visits to family friends. She preferred to read rather than engage in what she considered to be futile, meaningless social conversations. Her mother considered such behaviour to be unbecoming, impolite and disgraceful. She made every effort to convince Jyoti that her sole role was to serve the men in her life: first and foremost, her father and other male relatives, and then, in due course, her husband.

Jyoti had several cousins. She would have liked to get to know them better, but unfortunately, whenever they came over to the house, her mother would order her into the kitchen to make tea and snacks for them. If she refused, her mother would pinch her viciously and insist. If she refused again, she would receive a slap on the face. As she grew older, though, she learned how to deal with her mother's anger. In true Gandhian style, she would offer passive resistance. Irrespective of how many pinches and slaps she received, she would refuse to follow her mother's orders. Eventually in deep frustration, her mother would burst into tears and banish the girl to her room upstairs. Puberty made Jyoti's isolation even greater. She dreaded the time of the month when she was menstruating, because when this occurred she was considered an untouchable. She was not allowed to open the fridge or enter the kitchen. She was forbidden to go to the temple, and she was excluded from receiving the prasad after the daily prayers. The only redeeming aspect was that she was not expected to cook or serve any food. That was a great relief!

WITH SUCH A DRAGON of a mother, Jyoti's childhood remained a lonely and difficult one. Her father had no time for her, being too busy with his business ventures. Her loneliness was sealed at the age of thirteen when she developed rheumatic fever. The illness left her partially crippled and unable to walk any distance without crutches. Unable to see any improvement resulting from the treatments prescribed by medical doctors, Jyoti's parents turned to religious healing. A local swami was known to visit families in the area and perform 'spiritual' procedures to heal various ailments. The swami was treating Jyoti's friend Heena, who was her neighbour and suffered from some unspecified illness. The swami's method was to force Heena to have regular steam baths, which he supervised. The teenage girl would have to strip off all her clothes, wrap herself in a sheet, and enter a box-shaped steam bath. No resistance was possible since this procedure was approved by her parents and would be undertaken under her mother's watchful eye.

    Jyoti had heard from other young girls in the neighbourhood that the swami was a pervert. He had exposed himself to some of her friends, and whenever he visited their houses, would insist that the girls sit on his lap, whereupon he would squeeze them hard, pretending this was some sort of spiritual healing procedure. In spite of Jyoti's protests, her mother insisted on inviting the swami over to their house, treating him with great respect, touching his feet, and begging him to cure the crippled girl. The swami's visits became a weekly occurrence. Every time he came, he would grab Jyoti, force her to sit on his lap, and squeeze her tightly against himself. After his first few visits, Jyoti could take it no more and complained about the swami's lecherous behaviour to her parents. Her father looked surprised, but her mother grabbed her by the hair and slapped her hard. How dare she make such blasphemous allegations against a man of religion! Jyoti was accused of lying and making up stories against a good man who was trying to help her. Such was the hold of religion and ritual that no word of criticism could uttered against a person who wore the sacred saffron clothes. That he was an itinerant mendicant from some province of eastern India, far away from Gujarat, also did not seem to make any difference to the homage he was offered. Many months later, however, Heena developed obvious symptoms of epilepsy, and her parents then decided that the swami's ministrations were of no value. The steam baths were discontinued, and the swami's visits to Jyoti's house also suspended. No fault or blame was ever ascribed to the swami for Heena's epilepsy.

ALKAPURI WAS A VERY orthodox community. The daily life of all the residents was dominated by a predetermined and age-old cycle of ritual and religious belief. The morality or immorality of a person was not defined by their behaviour in personal, social or business relationships, but by their strict observance of the ritualistic requirements of religion. After the morning bath, diyas would be lit, prayers uttered and prasad distributed to family members. In addition, the men had mini-temples at their businesses, and the day could not commence without another round of diyas and prayers. There was deep and complete conviction that any deviation from such practices could result in bad luck, or worse. From the ritualistic point of view, the month of Shravan was one of the most important events of the year. Shravan was around July. The entire month was dedicated to Lord Shiva. Worshipping him was said to bring the most auspicious results and blessings of all the gods. Daily fasting would be observed throughout the month, with only a very limited range of vegetarian foods being permitted in the diet. One was expected to go to the temple and also make special offerings to Lord Shiva through puja at home every day.

Disabilities, and her mother's strictness, meant that Jyoti did not get out of the house much. Consequently, she loved social festivals such as Navratri and Diwali when celebrations were held at the local temple, and she got the opportunity to mix with her cousins and friends. Navratri consisted of many events, the most exciting of which was the nine nights of dandiya ras at the temple hall. Of course, she couldn't dance, but it was so thrilling to watch the women in their flowing ghagras twirling around the floor, hitting the sticks held in their hands against those held by their fellow dancers with greater and greater vigour as the night progressed. And when one of the dancers came over to where she was sitting and tapped the dandiya sticks she was waving above her head, she would be over the moon with pleasure and excitement. Other religious events, though, she hated. Her mother forced her to observe Gauri Vrat during the Hindu month of Ashadha (July–August). This was considered an important ritual to be performed by unmarried women and young girls. Legend had it that the Goddess Parvati had performed this fast to get Lord Shiva as her husband. Therefore, it was believed that by performing this ritual a girl would get an ideal husband. Jyoti had no choice but to observe the required partial fasts, perform the pujas, avoid salt and only eat foods made from wheat flour, ghee and milk. The diet made her feel revulsion for milk and milk products for the rest of her life.

RHEUMATOID ARTHRITIS ALSO MEANT that after returning home from school, Jyoti could not go out and play like normal children. So apart from the time she spent on her school work, and devouring book after book – on whatever subject – she could lay her hands on, she would sit on the first-floor terrace veranda, observing the dramas in the lives of her neighbours unfolding before her. Their immediate neighbour was Rasik Trivedi. Rasik kaka (uncle) was also a Brahmin, and a deeply religious man. He went overboard in terms of his ritualistic duties, and was highly regarded in the community because of this. The fact that he had two wives somehow did not seem to have affected his respectability in any way. His first wife, now in her fifties, had never borne him any children, and so about ten years ago he had married a second wife – a much younger lady. The elder wife had retreated into the safe space of prayer and religious ritual. The younger wife had borne him a son. So everything was perfect in that household. Jyoti hated Rasik kaka because he openly ogled at her, as he did all the other young girls in the neighbourhood. Nobody seemed to notice or object to such behaviour.

Across the street lived one of the few outsiders in Alkapuri. Shantaben and her family were from the fashionable city of Bombay in Maharashtra. Bombay was of course the home to Bollywood, the Indian film industry. Shantaben was in her thirties and married to a respectable businessman. She had two young children. Her husband looked much older than her: balding and sporting a big paunch. She, on the other hand, was very fashion conscious. She made up her face carefully every day and wore clothes of the latest design. She made every effort to look like a Bollywood star. Nevertheless, she seemed to be a very devoted wife, cooking and cleaning the house, taking care of the kids, and of course performing all the required religious rituals. One day, Jyoti, observing from her terrace, noticed she had a male visitor. Nothing unusual, thought Jyoti, but kept watching. The man was seated in the living room, and was offered tea and snacks. At first Shantaben sat opposite him, but then she went to the mirror on the wall as if to comb her hair. The man then got up, walked up behind her, and put his arms around her waist! Shantaben then leaned back against him and rested her head on his shoulder. Jyoti was shocked. The respectable Shantaben was having an affair with a younger man! In the following few months, Jyoti saw the man visit Shantaben again a few times. And then one day Shantaben disappeared, leaving her husband and two kids behind. The talk amongst the women was, 'Well, what can you expect of a woman from Bombay, so obsessed with her clothes and looks.' Nevertheless, the whole community was horrified by this act of gross infidelity and immorality. Jyoti never saw Shantaben again.

And so the years rolled by for Jyoti in Alkapuri. The requirements of custom and respectability ruled the social lives of her family, and that of the community around her. Jyoti had no issue with the community practising its rituals since it clearly gave them a strong feeling of being closer to the divine, and made them happy. But she hated the double standards being practised by many of her neighbours, and hoped that one day she could live in an environment where truth and morality mattered. She could not understand how greed, lechery, infidelity and other vices could be acceptable so long as they did not challenge the traditional way of life.

After completing her school, Jyoti was sent to Baroda University, where she completed a degree in sociology. She enjoyed her studies, loved her books, and did consistently well in her exams. She also grew physically stronger. Although she still looked thin and scrawny, she overcame her disabilities, could walk without crutches, and pursued her daily activities quite normally. Soon after her final exams, her father informed her that due to the expansion of their business, it had become necessary to set up a head office in the capital, New Delhi, and that the family would be moving there soon. Jyoti was overjoyed to hear that they were leaving Baroda. She had very few friends there. She hated almost all of her mother's relatives, who treated her as if she did not exist. Her neighbours she despised for their disdain of any true values and the open hypocrisy in the conduct of their lives.

IN THE SUMMER OF 1973, about the same time that Arjun was returning from Oxford, Jyoti found herself settled in their new house in Delhi. Her father, now a rich industrialist, had bought a bungalow in the posh Delhi neighbourhood of Jor Bagh. The bungalow stood just across the road from Lodhi Gardens, a beautiful park in which stood the tombs of the Muslim sultans of Delhi from the fourteenth and fifteenth centuries. Jyoti loved New Delhi – the broad avenues, tree-lined roads and spacious houses, all designed by the British architect Edwin Lutyens. Lodhi Gardens itself was so beautiful. There she would go for walks regularly, and sit in quiet contemplation under the high domes of the many tombs in the park. It was all so peaceful compared to Alkapuri, where everyone was crammed into a small area and literally falling over each other.

Since Jyoti had finished her university degree, her mother was now keen that she be married. As per tradition, this would of course have to be an arranged marriage, with her parents choosing a suitable bridegroom from the same caste. Jyoti hated the idea of getting married. Luckily, her physical condition and appearance were such that the family could not find many suitors. Attracted by her father's wealth, several Gujarati Brahmin families did come over with their sons to inspect the potential bride, but one look at her and they all politely turned her down.

After six months of sitting at home and being subjected to periodic inspections from potential marriage partners, Jyoti finally convinced her father to let her work. Given her own illnesses and difficult childhood, she felt it would give her a great deal of satisfaction if she could work with children who had disabilities. She wanted to make a difference to the lives of others, and the idea of working with the disabled strongly appealed to her. Through the newspapers, she had found out about a non-profit organization that had a home and school for such kids in the nearby suburb of Nizamuddin. She had visited the school, liked the management, and indicated to them that she would seek her parents' approval to come and work for them. The salary was not much, but this did not matter to her. She was doing it as a passion, not for the money. And so, in late 1973, Jyoti became a social worker at an institution for the disabled. Her daily life was routine and uneventful. She was out of the house the whole day, away from her nagging mother, and doing the kind of work she loved to do. Life was just beginning, she thought.

And then came the chance encounter with Arjun on the night that the Emergency was declared. She was intrigued by Arjun, but never expected to see him again. Little did she know that the momentous events following the declaration of the Emergency on 26 June 1975 would throw her life into tumult and challenge her humdrum daily existence.

It was early evening in October 1975. Jyoti had finished with her tasks at the school. The suburb was alive with people visiting the dargah of Hazrat Nizamuddin Auliya, the thirteenth-century Sufi saint after whom the settlement had been named. Jyoti was deeply inspired by the Sufi teachings, which emphasized an unconditional love for humanity. She was passing one of the many tandoor and kebab eateries opposite the dargah when she spotted Arjun inside one of them. Being a vegetarian, the idea of entering such an establishment, with its open display of raw meats, did not appeal to her. So she stood outside, waved at him, and shouted out his name. Arjun wondered who this wild-looking woman with curly hair was, but then recognized her from Sundeep's party and came out to greet her.

'What a surprise to see you again!' said Jyoti. 'What are you doing here in Nizamuddin?'

'There is a group of students from Delhi University who are angry about the atrocities being committed by the Congress government, and so I come here regularly to discuss matters, give them literature, and advise them on anti-government tactics,' replied Arjun.

'That sounds very exciting,' said Jyoti. 'I am not much of an activist, but I would like to come and listen to your group, if that would be possible.'

'Of course!' exclaimed Arjun. 'It would be wonderful to have you there with us. The more people we can mobilize to oppose Mrs Gandhi, the better.'

So Jyoti became a regular participant in the CPI (ML)'s activist group in Nizamuddin. She was not entirely comfortable with the language of violence expressed in the group. But none of the members seemed to be participating in anything violent, and she was very comfortable with the anti-government wall writing, leafleting and literature distribution that were the focus of their activities. She particularly enjoyed the honest and open debate in the group on a wide range of economic and social issues. Although sceptical about the communist ideology of the group, after the first few meetings Jyoti felt inspired by the anti-government commitment of the group members to offer her own services to the CPI (ML). Arjun warned her of the dangers of participating in any public activities. They could get her beaten up and even thrown into prison. But Jyoti was adamant that she wanted to contribute in some way. Arjun therefore gave her the task of ferrying CPI (ML) leaflets, posters and other literature from the safe house in Nizamuddin to party cells in other parts of south Delhi. Soon she was carrying this material to sympathizers and activists in JNU, Tughlakabad and even as far as workers' colonies in Badarpur on the Haryana border. The police never once suspected that this emaciated girl was carrying inflammatory literature calling for the overthrow of the government. Jyoti had now become a courier for the revolution.

11

The Emergency

THE DECLARATION OF THE Emergency was a culmination of the authoritarian measures instituted by Mrs Gandhi since becoming prime minister in 1971. Prior to the 1970s, the resilience of the political institutions established under the Constitution had never been tested. This was because the Congress Party had won a majority in all the elections held since Independence. Then came the split in this party in 1969 and the expulsion of Indira Gandhi from the Congress. Faced with this precarious political situation, Mrs Gandhi declared her splinter group's slogan: 'Garibi Hatao' – 'Eliminate Poverty'. Her electoral campaign was successful, and under this slogan, she fought and won a landslide victory in the March 1971 elections.

After this win at the polls, Mrs Gandhi led the country to a victory in the war against Pakistan – a war that resulted in the creation of Bangladesh. Her admirers now began to tout her as the new saviour of India, an avatar of Goddess Durga, the vanquisher of all. However, in spite of a few populist measures such as the abolition of the privy purses of ex-feudals and the nationalization of all the large banks, little else was done. The state of the economy continued to worsen. Unemployment and inflation reached new heights. In just one state, Bihar, the total number of unemployed graduates had reached 66,000 in 1972. Inspired by the events in Naxalbari, agrarian clashes were escalating all over eastern and central India. The early part of 1973 saw increased militancy amongst the urban working classes as well. Industrial actions and strikes were beginning to occur all over the country. Then, in May of the same year, in Lucknow, the paramilitary Provincial Armed Constabulary refused to follow orders, and revolted against poor pay and service conditions. Mrs Gandhi blamed the political opposition for the unrest and upheavals in the country. In fact, they were just the people's response to unemployment, high inflation, widespread corruption and bad governance.

The Congress government's response to this unrest was increased repression, harsh police action against protestors, and efforts to derail democratic processes. Mrs Gandhi was particularly keen to suppress the independence and power of the judiciary, which had ruled against the legality of several of her policies. In April 1973, her government approached the Supreme Court, and in the Kesavananda Bharati case, argued that the elected Parliament had the absolute right to change any part of the Constitution. Luckily for the future of democracy in India, the majority of the justices, led by Justice H.R. Khanna, ruled against the government and indicated that the basic structure of the Constitution could not be amended. Thus, the fundamental rights guaranteed in the Constitution could not be taken away through an Act of Parliament. Mrs Gandhi was furious at this judgement, and when the opportunity arose later that month, superseded Justice Khanna and appointed A.N. Ray as the new Chief Justice of India; she knew this judge would submit to her wishes.

As the economic crisis in the country deepened, so did Mrs Gandhi's popularity plummet. In January 1975, the Congress Party lost several by-elections in Madhya Pradesh and Haryana. It was becoming increasingly clear that the electoral promises made by her party were simply hollow slogans meant to fool the people. In spite of heavy repression, the movement in Bihar was going from strength to strength. On 6 March 1975, a huge procession of Bihar activists marched towards Parliament in Delhi. Mrs Gandhi and her coterie, unswayed by this show of strength, refused to negotiate with the people's movement and continued to use repressive measures to crush the dissent erupting in different parts of the country. Later in March, the opposition front held a massive rally at the Ram Lila grounds in Delhi. At this rally, Jayaprakash Narayan, now leader of the movement for Total Revolution, denounced Mrs Gandhi's government and openly exhorted the police and army to disobey any undemocratic orders from the government. JP called for a countrywide civil disobedience movement, similar to those led by Mahatma Gandhi against the British during the struggle for Independence.

JP's call for civil disobedience made many in the Congress fearful that their regime was going to be overthrown. The hardliners supporting Sanjay Gandhi now began to advocate a suspension of the Constitution and the declaration of martial law. These calls were reinforced when the Congress Party lost the state elections in Gujarat, and the opposition front led by JP was sworn in to form the new state government. It was becoming more and more evident that the people of India wanted to get rid of Mrs Gandhi and her government. Then came the final straw – the

Allahabad High Court judgement convicting Mrs Gandhi of corrupt electoral practices and disbarring her from being a member of Parliament. This was the trigger for the suspension of the Constitution and the imposition of the Emergency.

In 1971, Raj Narain, an opposition politician, had challenged the election of Mrs Gandhi on the grounds of a violation of the Representation of the People Act. On 12 June 1975, the Allahabad High Court finally gave its judgement on this case, finding that Mrs Gandhi had indeed been guilty of electoral malpractices. Her election as an MP was therefore void, and she was disbarred from standing for election for six years. Mrs Gandhi appealed this decision in the Supreme Court and requested a complete stay on the High Court decision. However, on 24 June 1975, the vacation judge of the Supreme Court turned down her plea, and indicated that while she could continue as prime minister until a full bench of the Supreme Court disposed her case, she could no longer claim to be an MP. Consequently, to save her position as prime minister and protect the interests of the small coterie of sycophants and henchmen with fascist leanings that surrounded her, a state of Emergency was declared the next day, 25 June 1975.

BY SEPTEMBER 1975, THE countrywide arrest of opposition activists and anyone suspected of being hostile to the government, which had been in full swing during the previous three months, was beginning to slow down. Arjun and Ram Sewak, in the meantime, were ensconced comfortably in the quiet village of Rajokri, near Vrindavan. With all attempts at protest being suppressed with an iron hand, indiscriminate arrests occurring under new security regulations, and freedom of the press being eliminated through censorship, the country seemed to have gone quiet. The regime was forcefully and quickly consolidating its hold on all the levers of power. Sanjay Gandhi, in particular, was becoming an increasingly powerful influence on the direction being taken by the government and the actions it was undertaking. By late 1975, the Youth Congress had expanded into a force of more than six million members. While the government had put forward a twenty-point agenda for the elimination of poverty, Sanjay enunciated his own five-point programme of action. The first point of this action plan was family planning, and under Sanjay's direction, the entire state apparatus was being mobilized to carry out this programme. His view was that the growth of population should be controlled at all costs. Targets for birth control measures were set for each state, district and subdivision, as well as for all the lower-level civil servants and government employees to achieve.

Based on a directive from the central government, the district commissioner of Mathura issued clear instructions relating to the family-planning targets to be achieved in each town and village in the area. Kanth and all the other teachers in Rajokri were summoned by the local magistrate and told that each one of them had a specific quota to be met on a monthly basis. If this quota was not met, they could be disciplined – transferred to a remote school or have their salaries withheld. The magistrate indicated that cash and other incentives, such as a radio set, would be given to men who agreed to undergo sterilization or to women who had contraceptive devices inserted. September went by without much progress in achieving the targets, either at the level of individual employees or the district administration. This angered the authorities and small penalties were levied on most lower-level civil servants and government staff. The lack of progress in family planning infuriated Sanjay Gandhi. He was having none of this. Orders were issued that going forward, more coercive methods should be used.

So far the upheavals of the Emergency had not touched Mathura district. But with the new government strategy to achieve the family-planning targets, this was to change very soon. Special vehicles were allocated to the health departments of the district administration. Accompanied by a police force, these teams would drive around the towns and countryside looking for potential victims to be subjected to forcible sterilization. The initial targets were beggars, pavement dwellers, itinerant traders and even lone travellers on the highways. They would be rounded up and taken to a makeshift sterilization camp, where after a quick operation they would be allowed to rest for a few hours and then told to go home. A family-planning certificate would be issued to them, which the authorities claimed would give them the right to food rations at concessional prices, etc. The advertised radio set would also be handed over. In spite of these coercive measures, the family-planning targets still could not be met. More strong-arm tactics were clearly necessary.

About 10 kilometres from Rajokri was the small village of Sahibganj. Unlike Rajokri, which was mainly an upper-caste Jat and Rajput village, Sahibganj was entirely populated by lower-caste Bhangis, Chamars, Kumhars, and Muslims. In Uttar Pradesh, since the lower rungs of the district administration, the police, and the paramilitary forces were mainly occupied by Jats, Rajputs, and other higher castes, taking coercive action against a village such as Sahibganj was obviously an easier option for the local authorities. In a pattern that was to be repeated in many parts of northern India, in late September, the village was surrounded by the police and other district officials. The personnel rampaged through the village, collecting every man and woman who looked of adult age. There was much screaming; children and adults ran helter-skelter, trying to hide or escape into the fields. In the meantime, a makeshift family-planning camp, with an operating theatre for sterilization procedures to be undertaken, was set up. The men and women were then lined up separately. Many begged and pleaded with the officials, indicating that they were either unmarried or did not have any children. A few of the younger-looking girls, who were clearly unmarried, were let off. But the boys were forced to remain in line. Then, in production-line style, the sterilizations started. Vasectomies, tubectomies and forcible insertion of intrauterine devices (IUDs) were the order of the day. By the time the camp had ended in the late evening, over 700 forcible sterilizations had been carried out.

The district authorities were very happy with the results of the day. The district commissioner would be pleased, the Congress leaders would be pleased, and finally Sanjay Gandhi would be pleased. But the tales of horror soon spread through the area, and even the upper castes were shocked by the brutality of this action. Kanth and other sympathizers of JP's movement spread word of this atrocity through their networks. Their message was that this was a brutal dictatorship that did not respect anyone's human rights, and that it was not just the lower castes who were targets of the family-planning programme but that no community was safe so long as Indira Gandhi was in power. The whisper campaign was the best they could do, as any open opposition or protests would have led to swift police action and arrests. A week after the incident at Sahibganj, a similar camp was set up at the nearby town of Farrukhabad. However, this time around there was resistance from the population and in the resultant lathi charge and tear-gassing of the crowd, many people were severely injured.

The people's resistance forced the district authorities to abandon this proposed sterilization camp.

THE REPRESSIVE MEASURES THAT were being implemented almost daily under the family-planning programme stirred Arjun and Ram Sewak: they couldn't sit by quietly while such terrible events were happening around them. There was little they could do in Rajokri or the surrounding villages. This was a rich peasant area, with little landlordism, and the communist movement, let alone the Naxalites, had no base at all. There might have been some sympathy for their ideas amongst the Harijans, lower castes and landless workers. But since they were living in the village under the protection of the Jats, attempting to mobilize the local poor was hardly an option. No one in the Jat community, except for Kanth, knew they were left-wing communists who believed in armed revolution. With a feeling of impotence growing day by day, they felt the time had now come to go back to Delhi and activate the underground network they had built over the last couple of years. The regime had to be shown that the people's opposition in the capital city was alive and well. Travelling separately by bus and train, avoiding the innumerable police check posts that had sprung up, crossing state boundaries on small tracks which wound their way through fields of mustard and wheat, they soon arrived back in the basti of Seelampur.

Shankar dada and some of the youths from the Krantikari Harijan Sangh welcomed both Arjun and Ram Sewak back into the basti. The news was not good. Delhi was under a dusk-to-dawn curfew. Although Harsh, their colleague in the Delhi Committee of the party, had escaped arrest, all the other lecturers from Delhi University who had collaborated in writing articles for and supporting the publication of *Janvaad* had been arrested. The magazine itself had suspended publication since Arjun, as the editor, had not been around in Delhi following the declaration of the Emergency. Harsh had abandoned his position as a lecturer at the university and become an underground activist, moving from safe house to safe house in Delhi. The police had raided his college soon after his disappearance, and he would no doubt have been arrested if he had been around. The only positive news was that the network of activists and safe houses that had been established in the past few years was intact and ready for suitable activation. A messenger was quickly dispatched to contact Harsh and ask him to come over to Seelampur for a meeting.

The Delhi Committee met the next evening. The group felt it was too small to undertake any open opposition against the regime. Such action would result in them exposing themselves and ending up in prison. Instead, their activities should focus on wall writing, distributing revolutionary, pro-democratic and anti-regime leaflets, and of course continuing to mobilize the working class against the government. The most immediate practical problem was getting hold of a printing press where the literature could be printed. Arjun suggested they track down the owner of the press where *Janvaad* used to be printed and see if he could help. Kailash Chand, the owner of the printing press, lived in Karol Bagh, a suburb of west Delhi. After making sure his house was not under surveillance, Harsh and Arjun visited him. Kailash Chand was ex-CPI. He had been in the communist movement for the past forty years. However, he had become disillusioned with the established left-wing parties a long time ago and was happy to help the new generation of activists. Since the declaration of the Emergency, he had also been keeping a low profile.

Harsh and Arjun explained to Kailash Chand what their intentions were and asked him where they could obtain a small printing machine. Kailash told them that he himself had an old but functional small printing machine, ideal for leaflets and posters. But it was too risky to operate this from the offices of his printing press. He was already under surveillance because of his past association with *Janvaad*. However, he was quite happy to loan this machine to them, so long as they could relocate and use it elsewhere. Harsh said this would not be a problem since he knew a group of Chamars sympathetic to the CPI (ML), who ran a small shoe factory nearby, and whose premises would provide an ideal cover for the printing press. So late one evening, two youths from the local safai karamchari basti, disguised as thelawalas (cart-pullers), carried the small printing machine, now well camouflaged with gunny sacks, to the new premises. Kailash Chand came over a few days later and explained to the group how the machine worked. There was much excitement in the air now. Their anti-government leafleting and poster campaign could begin.

For the next few months, an intensive campaign of wall writing, leafleting and posters was conducted. Once a week, the printing press would be commissioned and churn out thousands of copies of material. Myriads of slogans were raised in the posters including:

'*Indira Gandhi murdabad!*'
'*Sanjay Gandhi murdabad!*'
'*Tanashahi nahi chalegi!*'
'*Nusbandhi ko bandh karo!*' (Stop the vasectomies!)
'*Hathiyarbandh kranti amar rahe!*' (Long live the armed revolution!)
'*Har zor zulum ke takar me hartal hamara nara hai!*' (Strike is the answer to repression!)
'*CPI (ML) lal salaam, lal salaam!*'

The leaflets and posters were distributed widely through the party cells created in Birla Mills, Swadeshi Textile Mills, various industrial areas, and of course, in the safai karamchari bastis. The youths in the Krantikari Harijan Sangh did most of the wall writing, splashing any vacant wall with slogans painted in red. None of the slogan writers was ever caught. They would slip out of the jhuggi-jhompri colonies located all over Delhi, write a few slogans in convenient locations, and slip back into their crowded bastis. The underground structure was working flawlessly. The police were unable to make any headway because they were receiving almost no intelligence from their spies and special operatives. Arjun and Ram Sewak, who were known to them, were nowhere to be seen. They were constantly on the move, moving from one safe house to another every few days to avoid detection. The family planning and forcible sterilization campaign had made the Youth Congress under Sanjay Gandhi so unpopular that they could not penetrate any of the lower-caste and working-class areas to mobilize support or even gather any information on the anti-government activists.

THE CPI (ML) IN Delhi continued to carry out its activities in almost total isolation to what the rest of this party was doing in northern India. The tactic of 'annihilating class enemies' through individual acts of terrorism had resulted in the original party breaking up into several factions that were now operating independently in their own areas. The Naxalite squads in the rural areas had been almost completely wiped out in encounters with the paramilitary and other security forces. Occasionally, a representative of the Satyanarayan Sinha group, which was active in eastern UP and Bihar, would come over to Delhi with some party literature. But other than that, Arjun, Ram

Sewak, Harsh and the other activists in the Delhi region were very much on their own. Their activities, however, and the effectiveness of their underground structures had become very well known to activists in other political groups, who were continuing to oppose the regime under Jayaprakash Narayan's umbrella movement. Several key members of the opposition movement from time to time sought the safety of the Delhi Committee's network of safe houses when they needed refuge in the capital. This included many members of the RSS, Jat leaders, trade unionists, and even some of the religious leaders who opposed Mrs Gandhi.

One prominent group that linked up with the Delhi CPI (ML) was the Arya Sabha. The Arya Sabha was an offshoot of the Arya Samaj, the Hindu organization that did not believe in the caste system, and was trying to reform and modernize Hindu traditions and culture. The Arya Sabha was active in the Jat communities in Haryana and western UP, and was led by a group of militant swamis. Prior to the Emergency, they made a colourful and powerful sight, resplendent in their flowing saffron robes and turbans. The Naxalites in Delhi had got to know them through their participation in several mass actions including the Delhi bandh in 1974, called to support the all-India railway strike. The swamis had publicly declared their opposition to the Emergency and were now being hunted by the police. Through some common contacts in the opposition, they showed up one day at a safe house in west Delhi and sought refuge until they could decide upon their next step. Arjun and Harsh received news of their arrival and rushed over to west Delhi to meet them. In the safe house, they were shocked by the appearance of the swamis. The saffron robes had been shed, and in front of them stood two swamis with cropped hair, dressed in T-shirts, bell-bottom trousers and platform shoes! No one could ever dream that these were prominent religious leaders.

The two swamis, Suryavesh and Chandravesh, told their CPI (ML) hosts that things in Haryana and western UP were getting a lot worse. The government was expanding the scope of its family-planning programme, all civil servants were now expected to generate a certain quota of suitable candidates for sterilization, and if they did not, they were being punished. The police was also being increasingly used to coerce small communities into camps where both men and women were being forcibly sterilized. For such prominent religious leaders to remain underground while the people in their areas were being subjected to atrocities was not an acceptable strategy. They would look like cowards who were afraid of the regime if they continued to remain quietly in Delhi. Arjun and Harsh agreed with the swamis that though it was a difficult choice, there was no alternative but for them to return to Haryana and mobilize their followers to show open resistance to the family planning programme and the regime. However, they did propose to the swamis that while coming out in the open, making public denunciations of the government, and organizing street protests where possible constituted the right approach, they should adopt the guerrilla tactic of appearing and disappearing from public events, and trying to avoid arrest for as long as possible.

After resting for a few days in the safe-house network, the swamis did exactly that. They went back to Haryana, and for the next several months would appear, make speeches, urge resistance to the regime, and then disappear. Eventually, in early 1976, they led a large street demonstration in Kurukshetra, the town in Haryana that is believed to be site of the mythical battle in the Mahabharatha between the Pandavas (representing 'good') and the Kauravas (representing 'evil'). The demonstration was met with lathis, tear gas and rubber bullets, and the swamis were arrested. They spent the next fourteen months in prison.

Meanwhile, the CPI (ML) in Delhi continued its propaganda war against the regime, and when called upon, provided refuge to prominent politicians who were passing through the city and needed temporary safety. That was when Arjun came upon George Fernandes again. Like all other important opposition political leaders, Fernandes had an arrest warrant issued against him from the start of the Emergency. But unlike others, who either got picked up from their homes or courted arrest by demonstrating on the streets, he believed that members of his party should set up underground networks and oppose the regime. Between July and December 1975, he travelled up and down between Delhi and Gujarat, exhorting socialist workers to fight against the regime. He had chosen Gujarat as a base, because the opposition was in control of the state government there. On one of his trips to Delhi, he sent a message to the CPI (ML) that he would like to meet them. A meeting was set up in the safe house of a sympathizer in the middle-class suburb of Rajendra Nagar. It was felt that police surveillance would be minimal in such an area.

It was late in the evening. Arjun and Harsh entered the house and walked into the living room. There was a man sitting there with a turban and beard, clad in the saffron robes of a swami. On looking at him more closely, Arjun recognized him: it was George Fernandes, in religious disguise! The world had indeed turned topsy-turvy, he thought. The real swamis were running around in bell-bottoms, and the leader of the largest strike action that India had faced since Independence was disguising himself as a swami. All present hugged each other.

George said, 'It's good to see all of you alive and well. Others have been less fortunate. Many of my closest colleagues, friends, and even family are languishing in prison.'

Arjun replied, 'Well, we always believed, like you did, that the Congress government under Mrs Gandhi would impose a fascist dictatorship on India one day. So we have been preparing for this for many years. Look at the brutality with which the railway strike you led last year was suppressed. But now we have a well-established underground network in Delhi, one that will enable us to fight against the regime using all means at our disposal, such as the current propaganda campaign we are undertaking, and violent means, where suitable.'

George was very pleased by this response. He said, 'This is a tyrannical and illegitimate government. In my view, acts of defiance against it are necessary, and I agree with you that where the circumstances justify it, violence should also be used. After all, it is the state that is using extreme violence against us, the people of this country. So this must be responded to in kind. Of course, care must be taken to minimize the loss of life in any such action that we may undertake.'

Arjun then asked him what tactics or plans he had in mind and how their two groups could collaborate with each other. George explained that in the past few months he had established a small underground network as well. Through this network, he was hoping to acquire explosives such as dynamite. The idea was that George and his group would use this dynamite to cause explosions at venues where Mrs Gandhi was expected to hold meetings. To prevent harm to ordinary people, the explosives would not be placed where the public gathering was to happen, but be detonated at a distance, to show defiance and create uncertainty in the regime. George proposed that since the CPI (ML) was also willing to use violence in support of the people's struggle, such activities could be planned in Delhi as well.

Harsh and Arjun were very impressed by George's commitment and determination to fight the regime, irrespective of the dangers involved. However, they were wary of his proposal to carry out such individual acts of violence in Delhi. To them it smacked of the erstwhile Naxalite leader Charu Mazumdar's tactic of 'annihilation' that exhorted activists to commit individual acts of terrorism. Besides, tactically, such actions in Delhi would be unwise. Theirs was a small group, with limited capabilities, and such acts were likely to trigger a massive response from the state, which could result in hundreds of arrests, their underground networks being wiped out, and they themselves being arrested or even hunted down as terrorists and shot. After all, fake encounters of this kind had already been used by the regime to kill scores of CPI (ML) activists in West Bengal. George was therefore commended for his bravery, but was told that they would have to think about his proposal. In the meantime, he would be welcome to use their safe houses any time that he was in Delhi and to pass on any propaganda material for them to distribute in Delhi. A mechanism for the two sides to communicate safely was then agreed upon. Their meeting over, Harsh and Arjun left the safe house and slipped into the night.

Through their network, in the months to come, Arjun and the others were informed that George was staying in one or the other of their safe houses. They wondered how his plan to obtain dynamite and use it against the regime was going. To their knowledge, no such event in which explosives had been used to disrupt a meeting held by Congress leaders had actually occurred. Neither did they receive any offers of sticks of dynamite from any of their Socialist Party colleagues for use in Delhi. Then, in June 1976, George was arrested in St Paul's Church, Calcutta. He had moved base from Gujarat and Delhi to Calcutta, and from there had been writing and actively spreading propaganda against the government, both in India and abroad. He and the activist group that had been collaborating with him in Gujarat were arrested and charged with the possession of explosives, distributing underground literature, organizing meetings and inciting people to revolt against the government. George was put in chains and placed in solitary confinement in Muzaffarpur prison. He would remain there until after the Emergency was lifted. As it happened, George Fernandes and his group never acquired any explosives; neither did the CPI (ML) in Delhi. However, their activities were very similar. Arjun and his fellow activists could, therefore, have been arrested and charged with similar offences. But so far, that had not happened, and the CPI (ML)'s low-key campaign against the regime continued and expanded in Delhi.

12

Turkman Gate

IN EARLY 1976, THE family-planning campaign in Delhi began to intensify. Under directions from Sanjay Gandhi, this was soon combined with a so-called programme for the beautification of the capital. What this meant in practice was that slum and jhuggi-jhompri colonies were to be cleared and their residents forcibly sterilized. Officials and staff of the municipal corporations of Old and New Delhi were mobilized for this campaign. The kingpin of the operation, and Sanjay Gandhi's hatchet man, was Jagmohan, the chief executive of an organization euphemistically named the Delhi Development Authority (DDA). The modus operandi followed was that the concerned city officials would be summoned to 1, Safdarjung Road, the residence of Sanjay Gandhi, and given instructions on how to proceed.

Jagmohan had already commenced a programme of demolishing what were termed 'unauthorized' structures in different parts of Delhi. In July 1975, the DDA began its operations by undertaking the demolition of shops and buildings at Kalan Mahal near Jama Masjid. Twelve companies of armed police were standing by to quell any resistance. The destruction continued with the demolition of the Arya Samaj temple in Green Park in September 1975, and further demolitions in Karol Bagh, Arjun Nagar, and other parts of Delhi. The Shah Commission, which was set up in 1978 to investigate the excesses committed by the government during the Emergency, estimated that 41,252 structures were demolished in Delhi during 1975. The number increased to 99,073 in 1976. Violent clashes occurred between the DDA demolition squads and the residents of these areas. The old walled city of Delhi, with its predominantly Muslim population, was Sanjay Gandhi's next target. Government and other independent reports indicate that Sanjay Gandhi visited Turkman Gate sometime in early 1976. He was upset by the hostile reception he received from the residents of the area. It is said that he was also unhappy that the buildings around Turkman Gate restricted his view from where he stood, all the way to the Jama Masjid mosque. His mind was made up. The slums, buildings and other structures around Turkman Gate would have to be razed to the ground.

TURKMAN GATE WAS BUILT by Mughal Emperor Shah Jahan in 1658. It was one of the many gates that led into the old city of Delhi. Over the centuries, havelis and houses of noblemen and courtiers had been built around the gate, and further extended later, such that now the lanes were narrow and crowded. Around Turkman Gate, many jhuggi-jhompri clusters had mushroomed, and the narrow streets going in the direction of Chandni Chowk and Jama Masjid had been taken over by shops, small factories, and other commercial establishments. Islam, the sociology lecturer at Zakir Husain College, was from this area. Although most of his family had migrated to other parts of Delhi, he still had an aunt and uncle who lived in a dilapidated haveli near Phatak Teliyan, close to Turkman Gate. His aunt claimed ancestry going back to Mughal times. She insisted that one of their great-grandfathers had been a nobleman in the court of Bahadur Shah Zafar, the last Mughal emperor. She was always full of stories of past glory, which she told with great aplomb, chewing paan, her mouth all red, with regular discharges of betel juice into her ugghal daan (spittoon). Her husband owned a small shop that opened out on to the main road. When he got a job at Zakir Husain College, Islam had moved in with his aunt and uncle. Over time, sitting in the local tea shops, he had become acquainted with many of the residents of the neighbourhood, including several workers who worked in the myriad small factories in the area. The closest industrial establishment to his home was the Girdhar Lal Panna Lal Lace & Gota factory.

When the revolutionary magazine *Janvaad* began circulation in 1973, Islam took a few copies home with him. Some he distributed to interested lecturers at his college. Others he gave to the workers he came across in the lanes of Turkman Gate. There did not seem to be much of an audience for his revolutionary ideas in the area. Islam therefore decided to focus on the workers in the lace factory. He suggested to some of the workers with whom he had become friends that they call a meeting of their colleagues in the factory premises on a Sunday evening, when the owner was not around. Sunday evening came, and Islam found himself at the lace factory with a group of six workers who had come out of curiosity. He gave them all a copy of a recent edition of *Janvaad* that had a review of the condition of workers in the textile mills of Delhi – particularly the Birla and Swadeshi Mills – and then gave them a talk on how they were being exploited by the capitalists. He continued with a short presentation on Marxist theory, and explained how the current government of Mrs Gandhi was in essence a protector of the exploiters. That was why, he explained, he and his party advocated that the government be overthrown.

The workers looked sceptical. One of them said, 'Mian bhai, what you say is all very well, but it does not apply to our situation here at the lace factory. Do you know, this factory has been operating for a long time and my father worked here before me? When he retired, the owners gave me a job here. They are not exploiters, as you say. They are good people. The wages are not bad, and if we have a problem they are always there to assist us. For instance, when we have marriages or deaths in our families and are in need of extra funds, the company advances us loans. So we have the best of relations between the workers and the owners. It is almost like being one family.'

Islam was a bit shocked by this total rejection of Marxist theory and practice. But he persisted and said, 'Aha, but when they give you loans, it is at usurious interest rates and you remain in debt forever. That's how you are exploited and made into bonded labour.'

'On the contrary,' said one of the other workers, 'the loans we get are according to strict Islamic practice and are completely interest free. We just have to repay the amount received in monthly instalments.'

Islam was now at a loss for words. There was clearly no revolutionary situation here. The workers and owners seemed to have a historic relationship that was harmonious. He decided to move the topic towards the current government and its anti-people policies. However, before he could do so, Mohammed Din, one the workers whom he regularly met at the local tea shop, spoke up.

'I know you belong to an opposition party and have our best interests at heart. However, most of us here view Mrs Gandhi quite favourably. We like her slogan of "Garibi Hatao", and we believe she is trying her best to improve the condition of the poor. At least she has taken away the allowances and privileges of the old rajas and maharajas. That's a start, don't you think so?'

So the debate continued into the night, but Islam could not convince his working-class colleagues that they were being exploited and that there was need for a social revolution. Mrs Gandhi's government was also viewed as being progressive and benevolent, and in need of their support to bring about economic progress in the country. The meeting eventually ended amicably. Islam left feeling a great sense of dejection and disappointment that the working class had firmly rejected what he considered to be views that were in their own fundamental interests, and something they should embrace whole-heartedly and instantly. Nevertheless, a relationship had been established with the workers of the lace factory, and he continued providing them with copies of *Janvaad* and other anti-government literature from time to time.

The declaration of the Emergency in June 1975 did not do much to alter the views of those in the neighbourhood. However, the mood began to change as reports began to filter in of the forcible mass-sterilization campaign being pursued in nearby Uttar Pradesh. As friends and relatives came up with stories of the atrocities committed, the uneasiness grew. Islam's audience expanded. No one felt committed to any civil or other protest action, but Islam's views about the real nature of Mrs Gandhi's government began to gain credibility.

THE FIRST BULLDOZER ARRIVED at Turkman Gate on 13 April 1976, accompanied by a small police presence. Initially, some of the outlying hutments put up by slum dwellers in the very recent past were cleared, with no resistance from the public. However, as the days progressed, the area of clearance expanded gradually until even the homeowners who had been paying municipal taxes for years began to feel threatened. Then on 15 April, the Dujana House family-planning camp was inaugurated by Sanjay Gandhi and the governor of Delhi, Krishan Chand. Dujana House was a stone's throw away from Turkman Gate, in the direction of Jama Masjid. Almost immediately, rickshaw-wallas, street vendors, beggars and even passers-by started being picked up at random and taken to the camp for forced sterilization. In the days following its opening, Rukshana Sultana, a Muslim social worker connected to Sanjay Gandhi, started pressuring men and women of her community to come forward and be sterilized in return for cash and other incentives.[6] Soon the pressure turned into force, with municipal workers and the police being pressed into action to ensure that the daily target set for sterilizations was met.[7] Anger swept the Muslim neighbourhoods of Jama Masjid, Chandni Chowk, and Turkman Gate. A general strike was called. The authorities responded to this by increasing the armed police presence. The sterilizations continued.

Meanwhile, a more militant group of workers from the lace factory, who lived in the alleys around Turkman Gate, approached Islam. The demolitions happening around them, the forced sterilizations occurring up the road at the Dujana camp, and the increased police presence everywhere had now convinced them that Islam was indeed right about Mrs Gandhi's government, and the time had come to resist these attacks on their livelihoods and homes. A meeting was called in the factory on the evening of 16 April. Islam had alerted Arjun and Ram Sewak about this development and asked them to attend this meeting as well. It was 7 p.m. and an eerie quiet had descended on the area. Normally, the whole suburb would be bustling with people, plying their trade in the shops and on the pavements until late at night. Hordes of customers would be jostling with each other to get a glimpse of the bargains being advertised. But now there was hardly anyone on the streets. The bulldozers had stopped for the night, but fear of the sterilization squads was pervasive.

The meeting was surprisingly well attended. Apart from the workers, there were a few shopkeepers and homeowners from the nearby Faiz-e-Ilahi mosque area, whose houses and other structures seemed likely to be the next targets of the demolition squads. There were a few students from Zakir Husain College as well. Much anger was expressed against the actions being undertaken by the Delhi administration, against Sanjay Gandhi and his cohorts, and against Mrs Gandhi's government. There was unanimous agreement that the people of the area should be mobilized to come out on the streets and oppose further demolitions. Islam, Ram Sewak, and Arjun were asked to mobilize other members of their party and bring them into the area to support any action by the local people.

Ram Sewak immediately left the meeting and headed out to Seelampur. There he tried to quickly contact members of the Krantikari Harijan Sangh. He could only find three: Ram Lal, Om Prakash, and Birju. He explained the situation in Turkman Gate to them and asked them if they were willing to accompany him there to support the proposed protests by the residents of that area. They enthusiastically agreed. Meanwhile, Islam headed out to one of the safe houses where

Harsh was currently living. The 'Major' was told that his skills were needed at Turkman Gate. And so, by the evening of 17 April, the CPI (ML) group was ensconced at Turkman Gate. Harsh, having completed his big task of preparing a small stockpile of Molotov cocktails and acid bulbs, remained in Islam's aunt's house. Ram Lal and Birju were taken into homes near Faiz-e-Ilahi mosque, on the far side of the main Asaf Ali Road. Ram Sewak, Arjun, and Om Prakash were placed in a barsati on the second floor of a house overlooking the Turkman Gate police station.

On 19 April, the bulldozers started moving forward again. The people could take it no more. Protestors came out on the streets and attacked Dujana House. The police responded with lathi charges and tear gas. At 1.30 p.m., a large group of women and children collected on the main road at Turkman Gate to protect their homes and stop the advance of the demolition squads. The police started arresting the women and tear-gassed the crowd, followed by a lathi charge. Many of the women and children were injured. Undaunted by this, the protestors moved to the area in front of Faiz-e-Ilahi mosque and sat on the demolished structures. The crowd had now swelled to 5,000–6,000. But the authorities had made up their minds. Nothing was going to stop them. The bulldozers were ordered to move forward again. This led to massive stone throwing from the protestors. The conflict had now escalated and the armed police opened fire. Arjun and Om Prakash, standing on their second-floor barsati overlooking this war zone, saw many of the protestors hit by bullets and falling over. Suddenly in the midst of this melee, they saw Ram Lal run forward and throw a Molotov cocktail at one of the bulldozers. The machine immediately caught fire. The driver jumped out but the mob rushed forward and beat him to the ground. A second volley of shots was fired by the police. Many of the protestors around the bulldozer were hit. From their vantage point, Arjun and Om Prakash saw Ram Lal falling down. After that there was no let-up from the police. Random and repeated firing continued until the few remaining protestors in the area had dispersed and not a single person could be seen standing. The whole area was strewn with the dead and injured. Ram Lal was probably dead.

Closer to where Ram Sewak, Arjun, and Om Prakash were, another crowd had emerged from behind the Faiz-e-Ilahi mosque. They had seen the women and children being beaten and arrested. They had witnessed the police killing unarmed protestors at the mosque. In front of them was the old police station of Turkman Gate, manned only by a few policemen. In their anger, the mob attacked the police station. A few shots were fired from inside the police station, but nothing could stop them now. They charged into the station, chasing away or killing the few remaining police personnel within the premises. But their victory was short-lived. Reinforcements from the reserve police and armed police were already crossing the main Asaf Ali Road with the intention of recapturing the police station. This gave Ram Sewak, Om Prakash, and other protestors who had gathered on the roofs overlooking the police post their opportunity. Stones and acid bulbs were thrown from above. The weapons, though primitive, rained down on the advancing police parties, stopping their progress. Overwhelmed by this attack, the police retreated from the narrow lanes around the station where they were at a disadvantage. Seeing this, in a surge of adrenalin, Om Prakash stood on the barsati railing and started hurling Molotov cocktails at the retreating police force. He did not realize that one of the police commanders, seeing the rooftop fighters, had ordered his men to focus their firing in that direction. A bullet struck Om Prakash in the chest and he fell heavily back on to the barsati floor.

Ram Sewak rushed to where Om Prakash had fallen. He shouted for help; Arjun, who had gone down to the street to see what was happening there, was urgently summoned. Om Prakash was bleeding heavily. Arjun took off his kurta and pressed it against the wound, but the bleeding would not stop. He was in a panic. Om Prakash was dying before him and there was nothing he could do about it. Meanwhile, the police were continuing to fire at the rooftops. Bullets were flying everywhere and hitting the barsati walls next to them. Arjun held Om Prakash's hand. He could hear the police advancing again under the cover of this firing. The senior officers were screaming orders to their men. '*Aage badho, aage badho! Maro saalon ko! Maro, maro!*' (Advance, advance. Shoot the bastards. Shoot, shoot!)

What were he and Ram Sewak to do? Stay with their friend and revolutionary compatriot until the end, knowing that the police force was now out of control and would probably shoot them on the spot if they found them on the barsati roof? Arjun looked at Om Prakash. His eyes were closed and it wasn't clear whether he was dead or still alive. Arjun tried to focus on the situation and found that he was mumbling, 'Lal salaam, comrade, lal salaam,' repeatedly to himself. He looked down at his hands and saw that they were covered with Om Prakash's blood. In terror, he extricated his hand from Om Prakash's grip. Both he and Ram Sewak decided that the only option was now to flee the scene. They quickly jumped from the barsati roof on to the lower roof of the adjacent house. From there they climbed down to street level and started running. The advancing police personnel had now reached the police station. The mob that had taken over the station now fled. Random firing was occurring everywhere. Constables were firing their .303 rifles, senior officers firing their revolvers.

Arjun ran like a madman down the street. Ram Sewak had already disappeared down some byway. A mantra ... what he needed was a mantra to keep his sanity. '*Om trayambakam yajamahe, sungandhim, pushtivardhanam...*' – the Maha Mrityunjaya mantra automatically started repeating itself in his mind. He felt a bit calmer and immediately decided that he could save himself only if he reached the lace factory. Left, right, left down the narrow lane and he was there. He banged at the gate. Recognizing him, the guard quickly let him in. Outside, the shootings and brutal action against the protestors continued. Many of the protestors had retreated into the Faiz-e-Ilahi mosque. But there was no safety there either. The armed police battered down the front door of the mosque. Those hiding within were tear-gassed and then mercilessly beaten. In the alleys behind Turkman Gate, the police pursued the protestors. Many were shot as they fled down the lanes. A small police party entered the lace factory and forced the workers to sit in a line on the ground. Had any of the rioters entered the factory, they asked. The workers shook their heads. Meanwhile, Arjun was hiding at the back of the factory in an empty cardboard packing box. The police left. Soon, apart from the random shots that could be heard, all was quiet. That evening a strict curfew was imposed on the whole area, with no movement possible between dusk and dawn.

'I was in my house when I first heard the shots fired. I got up at once as I was anxious because my husband had gone to the Bagh ... There, I saw heaps of dead bodies and I began to search for my husband. After passing through that heap, I found the dead body of my husband. The way towards it was full of blood and dead bodies ... I saw other people at the Bagh looking for their relatives. I passed the whole night there. It was impossible for me to describe what I felt. Heaps of bodies lay there, some on their backs and some with their faces upturned. A number of them were poor innocent children ... What I experienced that night is known only to me and to God.'

This is the testimony of Ratan Devi about the massacre at Jallianwala Bagh on 13 April 1919. But it could well have been the testimony of a survivor of the atrocities that occurred at Turkman Gate on 19 April 1976.

In 1919, a platoon of fifty soldiers under the command of Colonel Reginald Dyer fired 1,650 rounds into an unarmed crowd. It is estimated that over 379 people were killed and 1,200 wounded. After the firings, the platoon left the Bagh premises. Relatives and friends then accessed the area, and carried away the wounded for treatment and the dead for their funeral rituals. The British government appointed the Hunter Commission to investigate this incident. The commission criticized Col. Dyer for opening fire without warning, and stated that it was indefensible for the firing to have been continued when the crowd was dispersing. Sir Michael O'Dwyer, the governor of Punjab, was also criticized for expressing approval of Dyer's actions. Subsequently, Winston Churchill, the secretary for war of the British government, openly condemned the attack and called it 'monstrous'. Lord Asquith, an ex-prime minister of the United Kingdom, stated that it was 'one of the worst outrages in the whole of our history'. In 1920, Col. Dyer was censured by the British House of Commons, and forced to retire.

Sir Michael O'Dwyer was shot and killed in 1940 by Udham Singh, a revolutionary freedom fighter.

In 1976, more than twenty companies of the Delhi Armed Police and Central Reserve Police Force personnel, amounting to more than 2,000 men, attacked the men, women and children of Turkman Gate, who were merely defending their homes from forcible demolition. According to the official reports, only fourteen rounds were fired and six people were killed. However, as the Shah Commission noted, there was a deliberate attempt on the part of the administrative machinery to withhold, fabricate, and cover up the facts relating to this incident. Thus, no accurate account is available relating to who ordered the firings, the number of rounds fired, or the number of people killed and injured. What is known is that the rubble and demolished jhuggi-jhompris in front of Faiz-e-Ilahi mosque at Turkman Gate were strewn with the dead and injured, none of whom could be moved because of the curfew that had been imposed and the continued police action.

Subsequent to the clashes, an army of bulldozers was sent in that night to finish the job, using floodlights. The bulldozers crushed and collected all the bodies – both dead and alive – and along with the rubble, disposed them off at a rubbish dump some distance away. The screams of those who were injured or trapped in the rubble could not be heard over the roaring and clanking of the machines. There was no pity, no respite. The bodies of many of the protestors killed during the rioting were un-procedurally and illegally carried away by the police and disposed of in an unbefitting manner. The demolitions continued for another ten days. Independent researchers place the toll of the massacre at 400 dead and over 1,000 wounded. Unlike at Jallianwala Bagh, the relatives of the dead had no opportunity to cremate or bury their dead. Unlike the colonial British regime, the government of independent India at the time did not see it fit to conduct an inquiry into this atrocity. The Shah Commission, which considered this event several years later, did name several individuals such as Sanjay Gandhi, Jagmohan, B.R. Tamta (commissioner of the Municipal Corporation), P.S. Bhinder (deputy inspector general of police), and others, as culpable for the excesses committed at Turkman Gate. But no action was taken against any of them, and no one was ever punished.

13

Doubts and Resurrection

AROUND MIDDAY THE NEXT day, Arjun donned a skullcap so as to blend in with the local population and left Turkman Gate. He headed for a safe house in the middle-class suburb of Patel Nagar. He was guilt-stricken, confused and in a state of depression at the events of the previous day, and had no idea where any of his party colleagues might be. At Patel Nagar, he gave a perfunctory greeting to his host, a party sympathizer, and then went up the spiral staircase to the second-floor servants' room, which had been set aside for underground activists. He shut the door, lay down on the bed, and fixed his gaze on the ceiling. The image of Om Prakash lying on the barsati floor, his eyes closed, gripping Arjun, their hands covered in blood, kept flashing through his mind. He had deserted his comrade to die alone at Turkman Gate. That was not how a revolutionary should behave. It was cowardly and despicable.

Arjun had been in situations where the threat of violence had loomed. That was the case during the gherao of the management at Swadeshi Mills. A serious clash with the security forces could also have erupted during the Delhi bandh, when the crowds he was leading confronted the police in front of Parliament House. But both these events had passed off relatively peacefully. Although he and his fellow activists were theoretically prepared for violence, this was different. Turkman Gate had been like a battlefield. More than 2,000 armed men from the police and reserve forces had attacked the demonstrators. Scores of people had been killed or wounded on the streets below the building where he had taken position. There had been bullets flying all over the place, with many hitting the walls behind him and one taking the life of his comrade-in-arms. Resistance to a fascist state no doubt implied that events like this would occur, perhaps with increasing frequency. But now he wondered whether this was how he saw himself, a foot soldier of the revolution, who like many others would probably become yet another unknown martyr in the struggle for freedom.

On returning to India and starting *Janvaad*, Arjun had felt energized. He now had a mission in life: to play a catalytic role in the bringing about radical political and economic change in India, a change that would improve the lives of millions of people. But as a small agent of history, he saw his role as that of an organizer, an ideologue, an inspirer and a facilitator, not a street fighter or gun-carrying soldier of the revolution. Perhaps that was also necessary, but he had never thought it through. Of course, an integral part of past revolutions – in Russia, China, and elsewhere – had been violent clashes between the people, led by revolutionary parties, and the armed forces of the regimes in power. Intellectually, he understood this. But at a personal level, it was a different matter. And he now began to wonder whether he had the commitment to go through with what this entailed, and if indeed he believed this was the path that would give him personal fulfilment. All these thoughts swirled in his mind as he stared at the ceiling in his little hideout.

Then he thought back to his conversations with Rachel. She had more or less accused him of being an anchorless person who had a need to believe in something. So his foray into Marxism and revolutionary activities was merely an ego trip, not a decision based on a worldview that he held with conviction. He had strongly rejected this characterization at that time. Since his school days, he had been interested in reading about and understanding the forces that underlay historical change. That was why he had chosen economics at university. But while he saw himself as a social scientist, he strongly believed it was not adequate to dabble in the subject purely from a theoretical point of view. To be a social scientist to him meant being an activist, using his knowledge of the subject to influence the direction of a society. That is why he had been attracted to Marx's maxim: 'philosophers have only interpreted the world, in various ways. The point however, is to change it.' What had convinced him further to embark on the path he had chosen was that this vision of Marx, and his key followers such as Lenin and Mao Tse-Tung, had not only provided an analytical framework to understand historical forces, but also elaborated the practical tools to bring about social change. This holistic structure appealed to Arjun's intellect and his desire to be an activist.

But then, he ruminated, there was activism and activism. One could become a full-time activist, like he was, dedicating his entire time and energy to a specific cause, to the exclusion of everything else. This, as he had discovered, required an overarching commitment to this path, such that all other normal joys of life became uninteresting and irrelevant. What Arjun was asking himself now was whether his desire to be an activist was so strong that it overrode everything else of interest to him in life. And did being an activist mean becoming a soldier of the revolution, participating in street actions, clashing with the police using acid bulbs and Molotov cocktails, and being involved in violent confrontations with various arms of the state? Surely the process of economic and political change involved a much broader range of interventions, extending beyond just mass protest on the streets of cities or guerrilla action in the rural areas?

What about the realm of ideas, he asked himself. The publication of *Janvaad*, the study circles, and most other activities that he had engaged in, until Mrs Gandhi had established her fascist state, had been in the nature of spreading ideas. In the two years until the declaration of the Emergency, these ideas had been the vehicle for mobilizing thousands of industrial workers, safai karamcharis and Harijans in Delhi. But to spread ideas, one needed a society where open political dialogue was tolerated. An open society that provided the space for spreading Marxist or other views relating to the emancipation of the poor was clearly a precondition and starting point for any form of political mobilization. Under the current dictatorial regime, on the other hand, the options were severely limited. One could attempt peaceful protests, but these would be met by force. And as had happened to more than 150,000 opposition leaders and supporters, you would be locked up in prison. So since all such dialogue and mobilization had become impossible, this left only the avenue of extreme violence as a vehicle of opposition to the regime.

Soon after the declaration of the Emergency, as a political group, Arjun and his comrades had agreed that their immediate goal was the restoration of democracy in India. It was only by getting rid of Mrs Gandhi's regime, and bringing about the restoration of such rights as the freedom of speech and the freedom of assembly, that the people's movement could be advanced. But the current repressive situation, and the deadly violence that Arjun had witnessed at Turkman Gate, made him think that perhaps there was a greater value in democratic systems per se than he had originally considered. At least in such systems people could demand their rights and would not be suppressed with murderous force by the state.

For the next few days Arjun remained in a confused state. Debates continued to rage in his mind about whether he was on the right track, the strength of his commitment to the people's cause, whether the communist state was the only mechanism that could emancipate the poor and ensure economic and social progress, or indeed should one be aiming to achieve an open society based on truly democratic norms. And all the while he thought these thoughts, the vision of Om Prakash dying on the barsati floor, and his own powerlessness to respond to this situation, continued to torment him. At night, he could not sleep well, and when he did fall asleep, he had nightmares. As a student, he had visited an art exhibition in Paris, and had spent considerable time looking at Picasso's *Guernica*. Now the images of the tortured and suffering people in the painting haunted him. He could visualize and hear the screams of the demonstrators at Turkman Gate being crushed to death by the unseeing and unforgiving bulldozers of the Delhi government. He would wake up in a sweat, but the images would not go away.

In the meantime, the party sympathizer Kamal Gupta, at whose house Arjun was staying, became increasingly concerned. Trays of food would be put at Arjun's door every morning and evening, but they mostly remained uneaten. Eventually, after the fifth or sixth day, Mr Gupta decided to intervene. Mr Gupta was a clerk in a government office. He was originally from Lahore, in Pakistan. During the Hindu–Muslim riots around the time of the partition of the subcontinent, he, his young wife, and his parents had fled Pakistan and settled in Delhi. They had lost everything when they fled and had barely escaped with their lives. Because of their experiences, they were strongly anti-Muslim and had become hard-core members of the Hindu nationalist organization, the RSS. Kamal was a regular participant in the local RSS shakha, donning the organization's famous brown shorts, training with lathis, and attending all the religious and political sessions. He strongly blamed the Nehru–Gandhi family for the partition of his beloved Mother India, and hated the Congress Party.

Rakesh, their son, who was a student at Delhi University, had imbibed all these beliefs. Prior to the Emergency, out of curiosity, he had attended one of Arjun's study circle meetings at Hindu College. His view of communists, based on the behaviour of the right-wing CPI, was that they were stooges of Mrs Gandhi, and an anti-national group controlled by the Russian government. Following the student agitations in Bihar and Gujarat in 1974, he had become an enthusiastic follower of Jayaprakash Narayan's Total Revolution movement, while remaining a staunch RSS member. During the study circle, he was surprised to hear Harsh, who was also a lecturer at Hindu College, violently criticizing Mrs Gandhi's government, and denouncing both the CPI and their Russian masters. His interest was aroused and so he decided to raise his doubts about the communists.

'Why do you people keep talking about Russia and China, Lenin and Mao Tse-Tung, and the revolutions that happened there? You should talk more about India, its history and great ancient civilization, and the heroes of our freedom struggle such as Rani Lakshmi Bai and Bhagat Singh. These are the inspiration for us now in the struggle against Mrs Gandhi's dictatorship, not your foreign stories,' he said.

Harsh replied, 'Of course we acknowledge and believe in the greatness of India, our ancient civilization, and our heroes. But the question is how do we go forward into becoming a prosperous and great society? Look at India today: poverty, hunger and deprivation all around. The only way a country can be great is if the people are free from exploitation, if they live in a society where they can keep the fruits of their own labours and become prosperous. That cannot possibly happen today with the landlords extracting everything from the peasants and the capitalists exploiting the workers. And over and above all this, we have the government of Mrs Gandhi protecting all these exploiters.'

'So what is your solution?' asked Rakesh.

'Well, for a start, nationalism, as emphasized by all of you in the RSS, is not enough. What is needed is a revolutionary change through which the peasants and workers come to control the state. That's why we talk about Russia and China, because that happened there, and so we need to learn from their experiences and apply them to India.'

Rakesh remained unconvinced. He said, 'You talk of a revolution that gives power to the workers and peasants. But this is just a myth. I don't know much about China, but look at Russia. The revolution resulted in the communists coming to power. They suppressed all dissent, and then established a dictatorship of their party. Then over the past fifty years they have become just a corrupt regime that enriches itself, not the workers and peasants you talk about. The communist dictatorship in Russia is not very different from what Mrs Gandhi is trying to impose on the people of India. That's why the Congress government seeks support and inspiration from Russia, and the Russian stooges, the CPI, support her. The Russians talk about socialism, she talks about socialism, and in fact so do you! I am not in favour of these -isms behind which you hide with the intention of establishing your own supremacy.'

'So what is your solution to the economic and social problems we face? How do we become a great and prosperous country?' asked Harsh.

'First,' said Rakesh, 'we need to dismiss any sense of inferiority and dependence on others. Rather, we must develop a pride in who we are, our history, and the potential we have to achieve any of our goals. Second, I agree that landlordism and other forms of exploitation must be ended, so that the energies of the people are released and economic progress can be achieved. But I do not believe that this will come about by having a dictatorship of the communist party. To achieve this, we need to build a democratic society where all voices can be heard freely, and people have the opportunity to influence their own futures through democratic processes. Third, we need to get rid of the Congress Party led by Sanjay Gandhi and Indira Gandhi. A new political leadership needs to emerge from the grass roots that has respect for all Indians, irrespective of their political views, so that we can work together to create a better India.'

And so the debate continued, with much disagreement, but with one fundamental point of agreement: that India did not need the type of selfish, corrupt, and self-centred leadership typified by Mrs Gandhi and her cronies in the Congress Party, and the need of the hour was to get rid of them. After the study circle, Rakesh invited Arjun and Harsh to come over to his house in Patel Nagar, meet his parents, and join them for a meal. Through several subsequent meetings, the young activists corrected many of the incorrect and hostile images that the Guptas had about the communist movement in India. But the Guptas remained staunchly RSS, and Arjun and Harsh vociferously continued to put forward the CPI (ML) views. Whatever their differences, they remained united in their hatred of the Indira Gandhi regime. Then came the declaration of the Emergency. The RSS decided to oppose this decree through demonstrations, sit-ins, and street protests. The regime met this resistance with force and arrested all those who participated in these protests. Rakesh, who took part in one of the protests at Delhi University, was also arrested. His father, being a government employee himself, made several attempts through his contacts in the Delhi Police to find about where Rakesh was being held and, if possible, get him released. He was, however, warned by his friends to stay away from such efforts. He was told that the RSS protestors had been arrested under the draconian Maintenance of Internal Security Act (MISA), and if his efforts to locate his son attracted attention, he could be arrested too.

Mr Gupta and his wife were distraught at the arrest and incarceration of their only son, and their inability to do anything about it. Sorrow soon turned into anger, and Mr Gupta then decided to support all those who were fighting against the regime, including the CPI (ML) activists. And so Arjun, and others who had gone underground during the Emergency, would seek refuge in his house from time to time.

MR GUPTA KNOCKED ON Arjun's door, and on receiving no response, walked in. He was shocked at the young man's appearance. Arjun had grown a scraggly beard, his hair was unkempt, his eyes red and bleary with lack of sleep, his clothes crumpled and stinking of sweat.

Mr Gupta looked at him with kindly eyes, and said, 'Arjun, I can see that you have been through a very traumatic experience.

But that is no reason to give up hope. If you believe you are on the path of righteousness, then you must persist, knowing that one day you will be vindicated. I know what you and your group are doing, and let me tell you that your fight against the dictatorship of Indira Gandhi is a noble one. Her sycophants say she is like Goddess Durga, but in reality she is the incarnation of the devil, destroying Mother India, destroying the soul of our nation. You may be a communist, but you are also a Hindu. Your name is Arjun, so you should heed the words of Lord Krishna from the Gita, when he told your namesake Arjuna that one must follow the path of dharma irrespective of the cost. The battle to restore democracy and rights of the people of India is going to be long, hard, and perhaps a bloody one. My own son Rakesh has been arrested, and we do not know where he is. So you need to gird your loins and ready yourself for this battle. The fight will uplift your spirit, and you will win one day. And when you succeed you will have the great satisfaction of knowing that your life had great meaning because of your participation in this noble cause.'

'But Mr Gupta,' said Arjun, 'I have just witnessed the death of one of my comrades, and on the streets below many more people died defending their homes against the bulldozers and the armed forces of the state. I felt powerless and I ran away from that scene. I feel like a coward and a fraud. I have been preaching armed revolution for the past two years, but when it came to a real conflict, I ran away.'

'It is not at all like that,' said Mr Gupta. 'There is nothing wrong with preserving yourself to fight another day. And insofar as death is concerned, let me tell you that I have seen horrors you can never imagine. Our neighbourhood in Lahore was attacked in 1947, and many of my friends, women, and children were killed before our eyes. We were just lucky there was a Muslim family in the area who took pity on us and hid us until the killing mobs had gone. Then we started the long and dangerous journey back to India. I will not bore you with the details but our will to survive was strong, we never gave up hope, and eventually we crossed the border to reach safety in India.

'So pull yourself together. Bathe, have a good meal, and then go and look for your comrades. I am sure they are all waiting to come together again, to reorganize, and carry forward the fight against the regime.'

Arjun could not believe what he was hearing. To him Mr Gupta was just a party sympathizer who gave him refuge in his house from time to time. He had never seen him an inspirational figure who had any strong beliefs outside his RSS ideology. But what Mr Gupta had said rang true, and it struck a chord in his heart. Arjun was indeed engaged in a noble cause. He was committed to it, and believed it was the right thing to do. Everything he had done in the past three years was not in vain. It had meaning both personally and from a historical point of view. So he was going to snap out this state of depression, get out of the house, and do what needed to be done.

Late that evening, after a hearty meal, he caught a series of buses that took him across the Yamuna to the basti of Seelampur. On arriving in Seelampur, he went straight to Shankar dada's hut. The old man was sitting quietly in a corner of the hut. There was no lamp burning to dispel the darkness. Arjun went up to him and hugged him. Tremulously, almost in a whisper, and fearful of the response, he asked, 'Shankar dada, where are my comrades?'

The old man was almost in tears. He said, 'Om Prakash and Ram Lal never came back from Turkman Gate, and we have no news of them. Ram Sewak is around, but he seems to be in a state of depression and refuses to speak to anybody. He has moved to another hut at the far end of the basti for safety.'

Ram Sewak and some of the other young men of the Krantikari Harijan Sangh were summoned. Arjun related what had happened at Turkman Gate. He told them of the shooting of Om Prakash and his own escape from the maddened policemen who were shooting everyone in sight. He told them about Ram Lal's heroism in attacking the bulldozer that was crushing everything in its path, how he had set fire to the giant machine and how he had been shot by the police in doing so. There was deathly silence all around. For the first time, the horrors of the Emergency had become part of their personal lives. Then one of the young men spoke in anger. 'They must be avenged. The government must pay a heavy price for this atrocity on us, our community and on the people of Delhi.' There were murmurs of agreement all around the room.

Ram Sewak then spoke. 'Yes, this atrocity must not be left unanswered, but the question is: what is the best way for us to respond? We are a small group of activists, perhaps not more than thirty or thirty-five comrades all around Delhi. We can form small guerrilla units and do what the Naxals did in Calcutta a few years ago – attack individuals or institutions which are part of Indira Gandhi's regime. But then we all know what the result of that campaign was. There was an overwhelming response from the state and a reign of terror was unleashed in Calcutta. Not only were most of our comrades killed or imprisoned, but hundreds of innocent civilians also beaten and arrested as a result. Our movement was completely wiped out and all our opposition to the state ended.

'No, comrades, no,' continued Ram Sewak. 'Vengeful actions will not get us anywhere. The Emergency has been going on for almost a year. There is very little opposition still active against the regime. The satygrahis and demonstrators from various political parties opposed to the government are already in jail.

It is up to us in Delhi to keep the flame of resistance alive, and this means we should continue our campaign of opposition while continuing to mobilize the people against the government. No rash actions. Rather, we should continue with leafleting, wall writing, small meetings in bastis and workers' colonies all around Delhi. We can support any spontaneous uprisings by the people as happened at Turkman Gate, while at the same time remaining underground and patiently growing our strength.'

Arjun and Shankar dada agreed with Ram Sewak. The young hotheads looked unhappy but reluctantly agreed that this was probably the best strategy to follow. Over the coming weeks, contact with Harsh and other activists all over Delhi was re-established. The printing press became more active than ever before, churning out leaflets and posters by the thousands. Wall writing became widespread all around Delhi. A group of two or three activists with brush and paint would emerge out of the slum they lived in, write slogans on the walls abutting nearby main roads, and then quickly disappear back into the slums. The police were at their wits' end. The bosses were angry. But no one was ever caught.

IT WAS NOW SEPTEMBER 1976. The forcible sterilization drive was continuing in full swing in northern India. But now there was also widespread people's resistance, resulting in police firings, and the killing and arrest of protestors in various parts of Haryana, UP, and Bihar. Towns such as Uttawar, Muzaffarnagar, Sultanpur, Basti, and Patna witnessed major clashes between protestors and the armed police. The Intelligence Bureau in Delhi had finally identified Arjun, Ram Sewak, and Harsh as the main organizers behind the wall writing and leafleting campaign of the CPI (ML). Many more plainclothes operatives were put

Doubts and Resurrection | 183

on the job to find and arrest them. Consequently, it had become much more difficult for them to move about on a daily basis and hold anti-government meetings in different parts of Delhi. Movement from one safe house to a meeting and then another safe house would only be undertaken after the route had been subjected to surveillance by some of the younger members of the group and given the green light.

It was on one such trip that Arjun found himself on a bus taking him to the old village of Nizamuddin in New Delhi. The village had become part of the expanding city, but still maintained some of its old flavour. The area was predominantly Muslim. The CPI (ML) had a long-standing cell in the area and Arjun regularly visited them to provide anti-government leaflets and posters, and to spell out the best strategy and tactics for opposing the government under the current circumstances. More recently, angered by the events at Turkman Gate, the group had expanded significantly. The newcomers had expressed a much greater degree of militancy, and had decided to actively participate in the anti-government campaign of the CPI (ML). The bus made a stop at Khan Market. Arjun saw three burly men with closed-cropped hair get on the bus. He immediately recognized one of them as the intelligence operative who had attended the meeting in 1974 when *Janvaad* was launched. The men were looking in his direction and he knew he would be trapped if he remained on the bus. So he waited until it had gathered a little speed, then in a flash, ran to the front entrance and jumped off.

The men rushed after him, but luckily the bus was now going much faster, so they could not get off immediately to pursue him. There was commotion on the bus with the intelligence men shouting, '*Pakdo, badmaash Naxalwadi goonda ko pakdo!*' (Catch the Naxalite goonda!) One of the men pulled out a walkie-talkie device and began speaking into it. He was radioing the police units nearby to converge on the area and hunt for Arjun. Arresting a well-known underground activist like Arjun would be a huge prize for the police. There would no doubt be benefits and even promotions for those who played a role in catching him. By the time the bus had stopped and the men had got off, Arjun had run into Lodhi Gardens. Behind him he could hear the loud police whistles of his pursuers. He was now in the middle of the gardens amongst the old tombs where the sultans of the Lodhi dynasty were buried. What a beautiful place to end it all, he thought, but then dismissed this negative thought and concentrated on how to escape to some safety. He could now hear the sirens of the police vans converging on the park.

Arjun was beginning to panic. The sirens and whistles were getting closer. This was a posh residential area, not a slum colony where he could escape into a maze of alleys and huts. 'Think, think,' he said to himself. Then suddenly he remembered Jyoti, the girl who worked at the school for the disabled in Nizamuddin, and who from time to time acted as a courier distributing communist literature to activist groups in South Delhi. Jyoti had once indicated to him that she lived in Jor Bagh, and Jor Bagh abutted Lodhi Gardens. In fact, he could now see this colony right before him. 'What was her house number, what was that number,' he desperately tried to recollect. And then it came to him: 117, Jor Bagh. He rushed into Jor Bagh colony: 99, 100, around the corner at 109, then into a cul-de-sac and there he was in front of 117! Without a further thought he rushed into the compound and rang the doorbell. It was early evening and he prayed she would be home. The door opened and there she was, the square-faced, strange-looking woman. Arjun felt a wave of relief sweep over him. He looked at her as if she were the most beautiful woman on the planet, an angel of deliverance.

Jyoti looked at him quizzically. 'Hello, surprised to see you here.' And then, seeing his worried expression, she asked, 'Everything is okay, isn't it?'

'May I come in, please?' he said urgently. The police whistles and shouting were getting closer. 'Of course,' she said, and led him upstairs to the barsati floor where she had her own little flat.

Arjun collapsed onto one of the sofas and said, 'Look, I am really sorry to drag you into this, but I am being pursued by the police and there is no one else I could turn to in this area. As you know, since the declaration of the Emergency I have been an underground activist and am now on the government's wanted list.'

Jyoti looked at him with the same intense, earnest expression he remembered from their first meeting at Sundeep's party. Then with authority she said, 'Calm down, you are safe here. I will make sure no one finds out you are in my house, and will certainly tell the police you are not here in case they come to my front door. While I may not agree with your communist views, as you well know I have grown to hate the current regime of Mrs Gandhi and her goonda son Sanjay. They have brought so much suffering to the people of India.'

On the streets, the intelligence men, the police vans, and their reinforcements continued to look for Arjun. But Jor Bagh was an upper-class suburb inhabited by rich businesspeople, politicians and senior members of the government. There was no question of doing a house-to-house search. So as night fell, Arjun's pursuers left the area, leaving him in the safety of Jyoti's barsati. He was so tired and emotionally exhausted from the police pursuit that he was soon fast asleep on the couch.

14

The Struggle Within

JYOTI HAD MADE UP her mind. She was going to allow Arjun to stay in her barsati for as long as he liked. Over the past year, she had watched with increasing dismay the dictatorial measures being imposed by the government. First, there was the suppression of the free press, then the constitutional amendments taking away all the fundamental rights of citizens, and more recently, the mass sterilization campaign under which even women were not being spared, with contraceptive devices being forcibly inserted into them. All this deeply offended her Sufi beliefs, her conviction that human beings should be treated with dignity, and that there should be mutual tolerance of one another's views. She had tried to transcend her situation of being a helpless observer by becoming a courier of anti-government literature for the CPI (ML). Now she was in a position to actively help someone who was willing to put his life on the line to oppose this fascist regime, and was reaching out to her for protection. Arjun's presence in her house made her feel she was not totally powerless any more, but in a position to become an integral part of the ongoing struggle in Indian society. So she was not going to refuse his request to provide him refuge in her house, irrespective of what her parents thought about this. She was a grown woman now and was not going to be bullied by her parents, particularly her mother. She was going to take a stand on this matter.

Jyoti's mother was in the kitchen. As she had done all her life, she was preparing the evening meal for her husband. Jyoti sat on one of the kitchen stools and said, 'Ba, I have something to tell you.'

Her mother looked at her irritably. 'I am cooking, can't you see? Anyway, what is it?'

'I have a friend who has dropped in. He is upstairs. Because of the Emergency he cannot go back to where he lives. So he is going to spend the night here.'

The old lady almost overturned the pot that she was stirring. She turned to Jyoti in shock, anger and disbelief. 'Wh-what are you saying?' she spluttered. 'Are you telling me you have a man upstairs? Who is he, and what do you mean by bringing a man into the house without our permission?'

Jyoti was undaunted. 'His name is Arjun, and I met him at a party some time ago. He is not my boyfriend or anything like that. Just a friend, and he needed a place to stay for the night, so I invited him in.' Jyoti did not want to let her mother know that Arjun was a communist or a Naxalite. That would be too much for her. So she said, 'He is a supporter of Jayaprakash Narayan's movement, and is opposed to Mrs Gandhi's dictatorship.'

All this was too much for Jyoti's mother. Her daughter was behaving in such a calm, matter-of-fact way and showing no fear of her that she felt unable to cope with this sudden rebelliousness. She turned back to her cooking pot and said,

'Wait till your father comes home and hears about this. He will put a stop to this madness. Wait and see.'

Just then the front door opened and Jyoti's father walked in. 'Listen to what your daughter has to say,' said Jyoti's mother loudly. 'This mad girl has invited a man to stay in the house. He is upstairs right now.'

Mr Bhatt had just come home from a tiring day at work. Business was not good. Mrs Gandhi's government was adopting increasingly anti-business policies, and the recent increases in corporate taxation were particularly burdensome to the company. These issues had been raised with the government by the textile business association he belonged to. But the concerned ministries were unsympathetic to the plight of his industry. Mr Bhatt was therefore angry and frustrated with the government. He was not in any mood for arguments at home, but given his wife's obvious state of agitation, he had no choice but to try and deal with the situation. He summoned Jyoti into the living room and asked her what was going on.

Jyoti replied, 'Bapuji, I don't have to tell you how wrong things are in our country today. The arrest and torture of people, the demolition of houses, the forced sterilization – even of women – they are all inhuman acts that cannot be condoned and must be opposed. Perhaps I cannot do much, but I believe it is my duty to support those who are actively opposing this terrible regime. That's all I am doing. Arjun, the man upstairs, is a supporter of Jayaprakash Narayan. I met him at a friend's party on the day the Emergency was declared. Earlier this evening he was being chased by the police and ran into our house asking for refuge. How could I refuse?'

Mr Bhatt looked his daughter in amazement. She had always been a shy, reclusive and obedient girl. This was a different Jyoti speaking. Bold, confident, unafraid and sure about what she was saying. She was looking him straight in the eye and forcing him to take her seriously. It was clear he could not treat her like a submissive daughter and order her to follow his commands. He then considered the situation they were in. On the one hand, this was a very high-risk situation for him and his business. If the authorities discovered Arjun in his house, he would be arrested, and even worse, his business could be closed down. On the other hand, he was indeed very angry with Mrs Gandhi's government and their anti-business policies, which were destroying the company he had built up so painstakingly over the years. He also had to grudgingly admit to himself that although he considered himself apolitical, he did not like the repressive measures the government had been subjecting the country to since the declaration of the Emergency, particularly all the restrictions on the freedom of the press.

He said to his daughter, 'Jyoti, I don't like the idea of this man being sheltered in our house. It is a danger to you and to all of us. But I do respect what you are saying, and sometimes it is important to take a principled stand. I am therefore going to allow Arjun to stay in our house for a few days. But he must stay upstairs and keep a low profile, and once he is confident the police are no longer combing this area, he must leave. Is that acceptable to you?'

Jyoti could not believe her ears. She had her father's support. She jumped up and gave him a big hug. Her mother, on the other hand, was most unhappy. She stood at the kitchen door, glaring at the father and daughter embracing each other. Jyoti quickly filled a plate with rotis and sabzi, and took it up for Arjun to eat.

Arjun was grateful to Jyoti. He said. 'You are just amazing! I never thought when I first met you that you had the courage and conviction to risk your comfortable life and support our cause in the manner you have been doing.'

Jyoti laughed and said, 'Well, neither did I. Your communist ideas scare me and I don't think I agree with the idea of establishing what you call the "dictatorship of the proletariat". I think all forms of dictatorship are bad and reduce the ability of people to control their own destinies. But I whole-heartedly support your movement to get rid of Mrs Gandhi and her stooges, and I decided the least I could do was to provide you with temporary refuge from the police.'

'But if you reject my communist beliefs, then what is your solution to the problems of social injustice, inequality and exploitation? How can the poor make economic progress and achieve social emancipation?' asked Arjun.

'I believe our aim should be that of establishing an open society,' said Jyoti. 'By this I mean a political structure which has rules that guarantee that people can freely express themselves, criticize those in authority as they wish, organize themselves to demand social and economic rights without fear of any repression, etc. So for instance, for me the answer to the exploitation of tribals in Orissa and Andhra Pradesh is not to form armed squads, like the Naxalites advocate, and then clash with the forces of the state. This gets them nowhere, just killed. The answer is to have a democratic state that is responsive to the needs of the poor and exploited, such that economic issues are dealt with effectively and expeditiously. I believe we need to have a constitutional democracy with well-entrenched laws that cannot be subverted by a dictator such as Mrs Gandhi, but which at the same time has scope for extension and deepening of these democratic rights. In such a system, people like you would be agitating for expansion of the economic and social rights of the people, not working to overthrow the system.'

Arjun was impressed by her conviction and firmness of belief. All the doubts he had about his own worldview, and the uncertainties that had crossed his mind after the death of his comrade Om Prakash, came to the fore again. Perhaps Jyoti, Rachel, Rakesh, and the others who had critiqued the communist political system, and argued for the establishment of open political structures, were right. Since the declaration of the Emergency on 25 June last year, he and his comrades had been fighting an open dictatorship, so he was keenly aware how debilitating a dictatorial regime was to the human spirit, and what a major impediment it was to any form of economic or social progress. And then there was the history of the Soviet Union. After the 1917 revolution, the so-called 'dictatorship of the proletariat' had soon degenerated into the dictatorship of the Communist Party, and later into the dictatorship of one man: Joseph Stalin. The brutality exhibited by this regime – the killings, the gulags, the general repression of the people – were now well-known historical facts. So there was no doubt that all forms of dictatorship which put restraints on thought and action were bad.

While Arjun continued to debate with himself, and with Jyoti, about dictatorship and democracy, a similar struggle was going through the collective mind of the people of India. Mrs Gandhi had been hailed as a 'goddess' and saviour of the people in 1971, when she had been elected to power after defeating the Pakistani army in East Pakistan, and declaring 'Garibi Hatao' as her goal. But this popularity had waned over the years as her regime became more and more dictatorial, culminating in the Emergency, and the arrests, killings, demolition of homes, and forcible sterilization associated with it. The people hated this authoritarian rule and were fighting against it, albeit in a sporadic and disorganized manner. They now wanted a restoration of their democratic rights. That was what Jayaprakash Narayan's movement was all about, and what Arjun's own activities focused on at the moment. The fight was all about re-establishing a democratic state, not ushering in radical political change led by a revolutionary communist party.

Increasingly Arjun felt that while he was on the right track in a tactical sense, his strategic thinking was flawed. The current struggle against Mrs Gandhi's dictatorship, using all means at his disposal including violence where necessary, was just and the right thing to do. But the idea of an armed revolution to bring about the establishment of a communist state was misguided. Ending exploitation and achieving economic progress could not be achieved by 'annihilating' landlords and other so-called class enemies, or by forming armed squads to fight the state. Rather, it required the creation of an open society based on truly democratic norms where everyone's voice could be freely heard and expressed without fear of any repercussions. He did not have to give up the ideal of achieving a just and equalitarian society, but these aims would be better achieved through a political system that was free from any form of authoritarianism or dictatorship, whether of Mrs Gandhi's or the communist type.

Having come to these conclusions, Arjun felt a lot more at peace with himself than he had been for a long time. The confusion, agitation, and depression clouding his mind since the death of Om Prakash at Turkman Gate all began to clear up. His only concern now related to his comrades in the movement. How would they view his change of heart? Would they not see him as a sell-out, a petty bourgeois revolutionary who had now reverted to his own class? Anyhow, this was not a matter he would wish to raise with them at this time. The current struggle against Mrs Gandhi's regime was ongoing and had to be intensified. Matters of socialism versus democracy were for another day.

Arjun spent the next two days in Jyoti's barsati. She would bring food up to him in the morning, go to work at her school for disabled children, and then they would talk into the night after she returned. Jyoti's mother maintained her angry posture and silent disapproval. Early on the morning of the third day, Arjun said his thanks to Jyoti and quietly left the house. He caught a bus back to Seelampur. As always, Shankar dada was there in the middle of the basti, seated on his charpai. Shankar informed him that Seelampur was no longer safe. In the past few days there had been several visits from intelligence operatives looking for him and Ram Sewak. Many of the huts had been searched and several young men from the Harijan community had been rounded up and taken to the local police station. Luckily, they had not been beaten or tortured, and had been released within twenty-four hours. It looked as if the authorities did not want to antagonize the lower castes of Delhi. Ram Sewak had already left the area and was operating with the CPI (ML) and other political groups in western UP, organizing resistance against the forced sterilization campaigns happening there. He had given Shankar dada a contact in Muzaffarnagar, and had indicated that should Arjun wish to follow him there, he could find him through this contact.

ARJUN MADE UP HIS mind. He would follow Ram Sewak to Muzaffarnagar. He had become a known figure to the authorities in Delhi, and it had become difficult for him to operate in the city. He summoned a meeting of the Krantikari Harijan Sangh activists and informed them of his plan to follow Ram Sewak to western UP. He believed he would be more effective there. He proposed to the group that they, and the thirty-five or so other activists in other bastis, continue a low-level propaganda struggle against the government. The printing press in Karol Bagh had still not been discovered. So a good source of printed material was available to the activists. Leafleting, poster sticking and wall writing could continue with maximum caution and without putting anyone in danger. The group agreed with his proposal. Arjun then packed his jhola with a few clothes and left for Muzaffarnagar.

He arrived in Muzaffarnagar the next day and immediately sought out Ram Sewak. The contact given to him by Shankar dada directed him to one of the Muslim slum areas. Muzaffarnagar had a significant Muslim population. On arriving at this address, Arjun was overjoyed to find not only Ram Sewak but his old friend Kanth from Vrindavan. The three of them agreed that since the regime was targeting Muslims in the sterilization campaign, they would spend their time mobilizing this community to resist this onslaught. Kanth introduced Arjun and Ram Sewak to other activists of JP's Total Revolution movement. Finding mass support against the Congress government turned out to be easier than they expected. The local Congress boss was a man named Vijay Bhushan. He was a good friend of Sanjay Gandhi, and had a very thuggish and bullying way of handling anyone he came into contact with. He had been extremely rude to the Muslim community leaders and told them in no uncertain terms that he expected them to cooperate in the government's sterilization campaign. The local district administration was also afraid of him. As a consequence of this, there was a general fear in the Muslim population of soon becoming the target of a major mass sterilization effort by the authorities.

They had not long to wait. On 17 October, a police posse entered the Khalapur area of Muzaffarnagar and picked up several men to be taken for sterilization. The Muslim community, with the help of Arjun, Ram Sewak, and the other activists, were ready for this. Resistance was organized and within a short while, more than 2,000 demonstrators poured into Khalapur chowk. The police were not prepared for this and immediately released the captured men. However, Vidya Bhushan and his cohorts were angered by this show of strength by the people and ordered the district administration to take harsh action. So on 18 October a huge force of the Provincial Armed Constabulary was assembled and the whole Khalapur area cordoned off. At 2 p.m., the district magistrate, Brijendra Yadav, entered the chowk to give direct orders to the armed police force. The police then started apprehending whoever they could lay their hands on, and bundling them into buses ready to take them to the sterilization camp. This provocation was too much for a group of Muslim youth who were hiding in a flourmill next to the chowk. They started pelting the district magistrate and his officials with rocks and stones. Many of the missiles hit the officials, including the magistrate. No one knows who gave the order after that, but the armed police started firing indiscriminately in all directions around the chowk. They then moved into the neighbouring Malhupura and Kairana areas, and continued shooting at sight anyone they could find. There was blood flowing all over the streets. Ram Sewak and Kanth had been in the flourmill when the shooting started. Luckily, because of all the machinery around them, none of the bullets hit them, and they were able to escape unhurt.

Since there was never any official inquiry into this incident, nobody had a precise idea how many people were killed or injured here either. The newspapers claimed that perhaps fifty people had been killed, but the true number was likely to have been much higher. Many Hindus were also killed in the indiscriminate firing. The incident and the mass sterilization associated with it created panic in the local Muslim population, and it is estimated that over 20,000 people left their homes in Muzaffarnagar to seek shelter with relatives and friends in towns and villages nearby. As in the case of Turkman Gate in Delhi, the incident showed the heartless brutality of the regime and its inherent fascist character. This incident intensified anger and hatred against Mrs Gandhi and Sanjay Gandhi all over western UP. However, given the fear it generated in the local community, there was little that Arjun, Ram Sewak or Kanth could do any more in terms of mobilizing the populace to resist the state. So a few days later, they quietly left Muzaffarnagar and went back to Kanth's village near Vrindavan. There, they kept a low profile for the next two months.

15

End of the Emergency

THE CONGRESS GOVERNMENT WAS in high spirits. In spite of the violence in Muzaffarnagar and other such incidents, they felt they were in full control of the country and had the support of the people. The secret reports being prepared by the intelligence agencies were totally misinformed, and gave the government a false picture that they were popular and would win any electoral contest. Since the term of Parliament had expired some time ago and had been extended without proper constitutional authority, Mrs Gandhi now believed it would be appropriate to call an election. This would give her full legitimacy to rule India. An election would also consolidate Sanjay Gandhi's pre-eminent place in the Congress Party and position him as its future leader. For all this to happen, though, the state of Emergency would have to be lifted or at least relaxed. Based on this misguided confidence, Mrs Gandhi announced the release of all political prisoners on 18 January 1977 and proclaimed that elections would be held. In practice, however, only activists belonging to the main opposition parties were released, while thousands of other detainees who were considered to be part of the extreme left continued to be held in prison. George Fernandes, who had been charged in the notorious Baroda Dynamite Case, remained in Muzaffarpur prison. Nevertheless, Parliament was dissolved and general elections were fixed for March 1977.

Under the guidance of JP, the released opposition leaders now began the difficult process of coming together and forming a united front against the Congress government. The negotiations were difficult, with deep-seated suspicions and egotistical ambitions acting as stumbling blocks to genuine cooperation amongst the senior leaders. But JP was unrelenting in his pressure on this group, and eventually they united under the banner of the newly formed Janata Party, with Morarji Desai as their prime ministerial candidate. Arjun, Ram Sewak, and Kanth, who had been living quietly in the latter's village during the past two months, were very excited by these developments. Here was the opening they were looking for to come out into the open and mobilize the people against the regime. Arjun and Ram Sewak returned to Delhi, but remained cautious, since they were not sure whether the arrest warrants against them had been lifted or not. A meeting of all the activists was called to assess the new circumstances and agree upon a strategy for the group. A message was sent to the Central Committee of the CPI (ML) faction that they were aligned to, to get some guidance as to the thinking of the party about the general election.

While the comrades were debating what their strategic approach to the elections should be, Harsh, who had now returned to teaching at Hindu College, was approached by one of his colleagues at the university aligned to the Socialist Party. The colleague indicated that the Janata Party wanted to field a single and united list of candidates in Delhi state to oppose the Congress, and that Atal Bihari Vajpayee, the Janata Party coordinator for the region, had asked for a meeting with Arjun and his group about this. Arjun was a bit befuddled by this, but the others felt there would be no harm in going and meeting Vajpayee and listening to what he had to say. The meeting was fixed and the threesome of Arjun, Harsh, and Ram Sewak took a bus to Feroz Shah Road, where Vajpayee lived. Outside the house there was a big crowd. Political activists, trade unionists, business people, fixers were all shoving and pushing each other to get into Vajpayee's house. They all wanted to present their credentials as the most suitable candidates for the Janata Party to select for the upcoming elections. The comrades looked at this crowd in dismay. Was this motley group going to defeat Mrs Gandhi and her henchmen?

While they were watching this unruly crowd, the Socialist Party lecturer known to them came out of the house and guided them in through a back entrance, where Vajpayee was waiting for them. Speaking in Hindi, he said, 'Bhaiyon, thank you all for coming.' He gave them all a hug and then continued, 'I salute you for your boldness and bravery in continuing to fight against the hated rule of Mrs Gandhi throughout the entire period of the Emergency. Now the time has come to get rid of this dictatorship forever and free the people of India from this burden. As you know, all the opposition parties have come together under the spiritual leadership of Jayaprakashji. It is time for us to work together to achieve our common goals.'

Arjun was impressed by Vajpayee. The man spoke with fervour and great eloquence. He said, 'Atalji, what is it that you want from us? As you well know, we are communists who want to bring about a radical change in the political and socioeconomic structures in India. We are wedded to the concept of the overthrow of this state and its replacement by a socialist state. We have very little in common with the Janata Party.'

Vajpayee was not fazed by this response. He said, 'We may have different philosophies, but at this particular juncture of history we have more in common than you may think. Mrs Gandhi has brutally suppressed all opposition to her regime. Look at your own group. You have had to live underground and hide in the shadows to propagate your views. Your ability to mobilize the downtrodden for any social movement has been severely circumscribed, if not completely restricted, by the current regime in power. Surely you would prefer to have a restoration of democratic rights in the country so that you can go to the people openly and spread your views? We therefore have a common goal today: the restoration of democracy in India. And in that struggle I believe we can work together by defeating Mrs Gandhi and her dictatorship.'

Arjun then asked Vajpayee what he was specifically proposing to the CPI (ML) in Delhi state, and how did he see this collaboration working. Vajpayee responded that he would like this group to become part of the United Front in Delhi state. A unified list of candidates was being put up to challenge the Congress in the state assembly, and as part of this list he was willing to offer Arjun's group six constituencies in the state elections. In return for this, the Janata Party would expect the CPI (ML) to campaign for all their candidates throughout Delhi state. In addition to this, Vajpayee also indicated that the Janata front would endeavour to have regular consultations, and seek the advice of Arjun and his group, on issues relating to the strategy and tactics to be adopted for the forthcoming elections in the area. Vajpayee's offer put the group in a quandary. They had always seen themselves as a revolutionary force. But now there was talk about joining electoral politics and forming an electoral alliance to defeat the Congress regime. This was something they would have to think about and consult others in the group before giving any response. Arjun thanked Vajpayee for inviting them to come and meet him, and for the offer of an electoral alliance. He indicated they would have to consult their comrades, and he would get back with an answer within the next few days.

THE GROUP NOW CALLED a meeting of all the senior activists in the Delhi CPI (ML) to discuss the proposition put forward by the Janata Party. By now Bose, the representative of the Central Committee, had also arrived and was available to attend this meeting. It was a cold January evening when the comrades met at a safe house in Badarpur. Arjun opened the meeting by describing the meeting they had with Vajpayee and the proposal he had made. He had hardly finished speaking when Bose butted in.

He said, 'Comrades, this is a dangerous petty bourgeois trap. We are revolutionaries committed to changing the basic structure of this society. Elections are a sham and cannot bring about any radical change. These elections are of no value and we should tell the people to boycott them. Armed revolution is the only path and we should not be swayed from it. These elections should be boycotted, and the people should be discouraged from voting or participating in it, in any way. That is the view of the Central Committee and we expect you to follow it as well.'

There was murmuring all around the room now. The manner in which Bose had spoken was overbearing and harsh. He might be the representative of the Central Committee, but the group in Delhi had never operated in this manner. All issues were debated carefully and finally a consensus arrived at, to which everyone was agreeable and committed. Laying down the law and ordering people to follow a certain path was not acceptable. Ram Sewak spoke first. He said, 'Comrade, thank you for informing us what the party line is and what the Central Committee wants us to do. We have fought against this regime for the past two years, based on our own strength and resources. The party and Central Committee gave us no support. While we may agree with what you are saying, we were not consulted in arriving at this position, and we are certainly not going to accept any imposition of ideas on us.'

Many in the group nodded in agreement. Arjun then said, 'Bose, we are all committed to the armed revolution. But without mass support and mass mobilization, this path will get us nowhere. We all know what happened to the thousands of our comrades who followed the misguided strategy espoused by Charu Mazumdar. Forming guerrilla squads and attempting to take on the state only got them killed and reduced the party to the residual group that we are now. Since June 1975, when the Emergency was declared, we have had little space and ability to spread our vision amongst the masses and organize them for the upcoming struggle. As a first step, therefore, it is essential that we get rid of the fascist Congress regime and restore the democratic rights of the people. In my opinion, if forming an alliance with other political parties and participating in the elections can help us achieve this goal, then we should not act in a doctrinaire manner and reject this opportunity.'

Some in the room indicated their agreement with Arjun. Harsh expressed his strong reservations and opposition to participating in the elections. There was clearly no consensus. Bose indicated he was leaving the next day to report to the Central Committee, which was now based in the jungles of south Bihar. He stated categorically that if the Delhi unit was not willing to follow the party line on this matter, he would recommend to the leadership that the group be disaffiliated from the party. They were then free to do as they wished, but they would no longer be part of the CPI (ML). He then left the meeting.

The debate amongst the comrades continued into the night. But after several hours of heated discussion, no consensus could be achieved. Harsh and some of the activists were strongly opposed to joining any united front with other opposition parties and participating in the elections. Arjun, Ram Sewak, and a few others, on the other hand, believed this was the correct strategy for the moment and they would be missing a great historical opportunity if they did not participate in the elections. Since there was no agreement, it was eventually agreed that each person was free to act according to his or her own beliefs on this matter. However, since they would be unable to operate as a united group, Vajpayee and the Janata Party should be informed that they would not be taking up the offer of putting up six of their own candidates for the Delhi state assembly elections. Arjun and Ram Sewak decided that since they had established a good working relationship with Kanth and other activists of JP's Total Revolution movement in western UP, they would revert to that area. There they would actively campaign for the defeat of Congress candidates and the victory of the opposition.

For the next six weeks, Arjun and the others travelled the length and breadth of western UP. They visited Mathura, Muzaffarnagar, Moradabad, and many villages in between. The message was simple. Mrs Gandhi was a brutal dictator who had mutilated millions through her forcible sterilization programme, arrested the innocent, and shot and killed many of those who had opposed this oppression. The people must come out in large numbers and vote for Janata Party candidates. The Congress must be defeated.

The elections were held between 16 and 20 March 1977. The results were announced soon after. The Congress was wiped out in northern India, with the Janata Party and its allies gaining a majority of the seats in Parliament. Mrs Gandhi and Sanjay Gandhi were both defeated in their constituencies. The people of India had rejected the tyrant and the suppression of democracy by her regime. The Emergency was lifted on 21 March and the Janata Party formed a national government on 24 March. Arjun, Ram Sewak, Kanth, and all the other activists were overjoyed with this outcome. They had put life and limb on the line to defeat the regime, and after twenty months, it had finally been defeated. One of India's darkest periods had ended. The goal of a socialist revolution was still very far off, but at least they had succeeded in restoring democracy to the country. It was a small but crucial step.

After the Janata Party victory, Arjun returned to Delhi. He had participated in a tumultuous election in which millions of the people had expressed their views. He had attended hundreds of meetings and spoken to thousands of people during the campaign. The experience made him realize the strength of the human spirit and the ability of the common people, though poor and perhaps uneducated, to overcome their fear and fight against adversity. It convinced him that what Rachel, Jyoti, Rakesh, and others had been telling him was correct. Revolutionary change, certainly in the Indian context, could not be brought about by a small, highly motivated group attempting to overthrow the state. Change could only come through the establishment of more open political systems, which allowed the masses to express their views freely and influence the direction of society. The communist ideal of a just society free from exploitation was a laudable one, but it was not something that would be achieved through establishing the dictatorship of the Communist Party. He could not subscribe to this idea any more.

Arjun was fearful of conveying his changed views and change of heart to his comrades. What would they say? At a minimum, he expected to be denounced as a middle-class weakling who did not have a commitment to the revolution and could not stomach the rigours of the struggle. But after all these years, there was no question of just walking away from the group. So he requested a meeting of all the senior activists in Seelampur. At the meeting he poured his heart out to his comrades. He explained to them why he no longer saw himself as a foot soldier of the revolution. He told them about his experiences during the recently concluded elections, which had convinced him that meaningful political change could only occur by mobilizing the masses in open and democratic systems. To his great surprise, not a single person at the meeting denounced him. At times Harsh looked angry and it seemed as if he was about to burst out in a fury. But the mood in general was sombre.

Eventually, Ram Sewak broke the ice by going up to Arjun, embracing him, and saying, 'My brother, you are a good man. We will be sad to see you go. Our struggle against exploitation will continue, with or without you. But I wish you well in whatever you do. You will always be with us in spirit.' All the others then embraced Arjun as well. After the usual meal of pork curry and roti, with a heavy heart, Arjun left the gathering. This chapter of his life was now coming to an end.

It was now June 1977. The Janata government, though ineffective and squabbling amongst themselves, had reversed most of the draconian laws and amendments to the Constitution that had subverted India's democracy and enabled Mrs Gandhi to rule as a dictator. Arjun felt particularly fulfilled by the journey he had undertaken over the past four years, since that summer day in 1973 when he had returned to India from England. Then, he had been a confused young man searching for some meaning in his life and looking for a way to contribute to the greater social good. Now he was at peace with himself. He did not feel it was necessary to be part of some grand political movement, with lofty ideals, for his daily life to be validated. He had contributed to something much bigger than himself, and that gave him a sense of pride and achievement. The fight for social justice would continue. There were others who would continue to be the torchbearers of that struggle.

Epilogue

More than six years had elapsed since that scorching afternoon in 1973 when Arjun had arrived in India, full of revolutionary fervour. It was now July 1979. The flight from Bombay to Delhi was full. Arjun had been wait-listed until the last minute and then given a seat. He boarded and quickly walked down the aisle to his seat at the back of the plane. Next to him was a man in a kurta-pyjama. He could not see the person's face, since his neighbour had buried his head in the newspaper he was reading. After take-off, the man lowered the newspaper and Arjun saw that it was George Fernandes. George was now Union minister for industries in the Janata government. Mrs Gandhi had not released him during the March elections and he had remained shackled in Muzaffarpur prison. Nevertheless, he had stood for election from prison and had had a resounding victory, with one of the largest electoral majorities in the history of Indian parliamentary elections.

George, as always, was a simple man. No fanfare about him. He was dressed in a simple kurta-pyjama and travelling alone without any official cohorts in economy class. Arjun turned towards him and said, 'Hello, George. Do you remember me?'

George looked closely at Arjun, and then after a few moments said in an amused tone, 'Yes, of course, I remember you from the days of the Emergency. Still making Molotov cocktails!?'

Arjun laughed. What an observation to receive from a senior member of the Government of India, he thought. 'No, George, not at all,' he said. 'For the past year I have been working with the United Nations as a development economist. I work for a department that deals with the poorest countries of the world and provides them advice about how they can improve their economic performance and reduce poverty. As for the Molotov cocktails, we don't need them any more, do we? Just as much as we don't need the sticks of dynamite which Mrs Gandhi alleged you had collected and were ready to use in a bombing campaign.'

George smiled. 'At least we got rid of that dictator and succeeded in restoring India's democracy. No need for bombs any more. We have a free society now and must work towards entrenching the values contained in our Constitution.'

'Not such a free society, George,' said Arjun. 'We might have gotten rid of the tyrant, but there is still so much poverty and inequality.'

'Well, that's our next fight,' said George. 'But at least now the poor can be freely mobilized to make their demands, express them, and hold politicians accountable through the electoral system. And after Mrs Gandhi's defeat, politicians will be wary of tampering with the democratic rights of the people.'

'Maybe,' observed Arjun. 'But I am not so sure our political system will be able to eliminate exploitation and bring about social justice so easily. I think there will have to be a much greater intensification of the struggle by the rural and urban poor before these goals are achieved.'

So their conversation continued for the next hour or so until they reached Delhi. George wished Arjun all the best in his future work, and they parted ways.

Arjun was very pleased with this encounter with George Fernandes. They had both moved on in life, doing what they were best equipped to do: George as a political leader, and Arjun as an economist working for the poorest nations of the world. This thought gave him a great deal of satisfaction. His comrades in the Bhangi basti of Seelampur would always remain in his heart. Their inspiration would ensure that he would continue to support the struggle for social justice wherever his karma took him. India's people had also made up their mind. Through the elections of 1977, they had decisively rejected all forms of authoritarianism and opted for democracy. The struggle within had been resolved. Whether this would lead to the creation of a society where poverty and exploitation were being addressed, only time would tell.

THE JANATA GOVERNMENT COLLAPSED in July 1979. The Shah Commission, which had been set up to investigate the atrocities committed during the Emergency, came up with thousands of pages of testimony and evidence. But with the fall of the government, the effort to prosecute and convict Mrs Gandhi, Sanjay Gandhi, and their henchmen, for the crimes they had committed, also failed. Nevertheless, the Janata government did succeed in lifting the shadow of dictatorship that had threatened to overwhelm the people of India.

Sanjay Gandhi died in a flying accident in June 1980. His passing was not mourned.

Mrs Gandhi was re-elected as prime minister in 1980. The people of India seemed to have forgiven her for all the crimes she had committed, and for her efforts to destroy India's democracy. But she was never the same after the death of Sanjay Gandhi. And one lesson she did learn after the defeat of her tyrannical rule during the Emergency was not to tamper with the rights of the people again. She was assassinated by her Sikh bodyguard in 1984 in revenge for the attack she ordered on their sacred shrine, the Golden Temple.

Since the 1980s, India's democratic system has endured and strengthened. However, in spite of the huge advances made by the economy, the system has not delivered benefits to large sections of the poor and marginalized. From around 2004, a significant escalation of violence in the rural areas, particularly in the tribal belt, has been observed. Over 100 districts in a number of states, including Bihar, Jharkhand, Odisha, Maharashtra, Andhra Pradesh and Chhattisgarh, have seen armed conflict between the poor peasantry, led by Naxalite groups, and paramilitary forces. It is estimated that over 15,000 people, half of them civilians, have been killed in this conflict. The economic demands of the people in these areas are their age-old demands and have not changed. They relate to redistribution of land to the poor; full control by the local people over forestry, mineral, and other resources; and the provision of more employment opportunities. In 2011, Prime Minister Manmohan Singh said, 'Development is the master remedy to win over the people.' Unfortunately, this development does not seem to have reached the poor in these areas yet.

The struggle continues.

Notes

1. See also 'Emergency: Indira Gandhi, rubber stamp President Fakhruddin toyed with democracy to give India its darkest days', *My Nation*, 25 June 2020, https://www.mynation.com/india-news/emergency-indira-gandhi-rubber-stamp-president-fakhruddin-toyed-with-democracy-to-give-india-its-dark-days-qch02s, accessed on 29 April 2021.
2. See excerpt from Gyan Prakash's *Emergency Chronicles: Indira Gandhi and Democracy's Turning Point* (Penguin Random House India, 2018) in Manasa Mohan, 'President who took a tranquiliser after signing away India's democratic rights to Indira', The Print, 11 February 2019, https://theprint.in/theprint.profile/president-who-took-a-tranquiliser-after-signing-away-indias-democratic-rights-to-indira/190303/, accessed on 31 May 2021.
3. See also Kuldip Nayar, *Beyond the Lines: An Autobiography*, Roli Books, 2012; review of Vinod Mehta's *The Sanjay Story* (HarperCollins Publishers India, 2012) by Shantanu Bhattacharji, 'The tale of the original brat No.1', *Business Standard*, 14 February 2013, https://www.business-standard.

com/article/beyond-business/the-tale-of-the-original-brat-no-1-113021400575_1.html, accessed on 29 April 2021; and Ramachandra Guha, 'The living legacy of Sanjay Gandhi', *The Telegraph*, 11 September 2010, http://ramachandraguha.in/archives/the-living-legacy-of-sanjay-gandhi.html, accessed on 29 April 2021.

4. 'Broken people. Caste violence against India's "Untouchables"', Report by Human Rights Watch, 1 March 1999, https://www.hrw.org/report/1999/03/01/broken-people/caste-violence-against-indias-untouchables, accessed on 1 May 2021.

5. See also Arvind Sinha and Indu Sinha, 'Ranveer Sena and "massacre widows"', *Economic and Political Weekly* 36, no. 43 (2001): 4095–99, http://www.jstor.org/stable/4411296, accessed on 5 May 2021; and Sunil Kashyap, 'Thakurs unleash anti-Dalit violence in UP during the lockdown, police accused of bias', *The Caravan*, 18 August 2020, https://caravanmagazine.in/news/uttar-pradesh-adityanath-thakur-dalit-caste-violence, accessed on 1 May 2021.

6. See Sunil Sethi, Suchitra Behal, Shirley Joshua and Mandira Purie, 'Rukhsana Sultana: The chief glamour girl of the Emergency', *India Today*, 4 August 2014, https://www.indiatoday.in/magazine/investigation/story/19770531-rukhsana-sultana-the-chief-glamour-girl-of-the-emergency-823746-2014-08-14, accessed on 1 May 2021; also, Danish Raza, 'Tragedy at Turkman Gate: Witnesses recount horror of Emergency', *Hindustan Times*, 29 June 2015, https://www.hindustantimes.com/india/tragedy-at-turkman-gate-witnesses-recount-horror-of-emergency/story-UD6kxHbROYSBMlDbjQLYpJ.html, accessed on 1 May 2021.

7. See also Emma Tarlo, *Unsettling Memories: Narratives of the Emergency in Delhi*, University of California Press, 2003.

Index

Act of Parliament, 140
Ahmed, Fakhruddin Ali, 73
Akali party, 76
Ali, Tariq, 19
alienation, 20
Alkapuri, Gujarat, 127–28, 131, 134
All India Railwaymen's Federation, 39
All Saints High School, 83, 92
Arya Sabha, 150
Arya Samaj, 150
Arya Samaj movement, 56
Asquith, Lord, 167
Aurangzeb, Emperor, 89–90
concept of authority as threat to freedom, 20. *See also* Rachel

'Baaghi Ballia' (Revolutionary Ballia), 116
Bakunin, Mikhail, 19
as anarchistic, 33
view of transition from capitalism to socialism, 33
Ballia, 114–15, 120–21
landlord killings in, 125
landlords of, 24, 116, 119, 121–24
Bangladesh, 139
Baroda Dynamite Case, 198
Baroda University, 134
beautification of capital, 156
demolitions, 157
Turkman gate demolition and rioting, 157, 161–69, 171, 174, 180, 183, 192, 196

violence and clashes
following, 157
Bhagavad Gita, 79
Bhangis (or 'untouchable'
caste), 14, 60, 114, 116,
118, 122, 124, 144, 209.
See also Harijan basti of
Shahdara
Bhinder, P.S. (Deputy
Inspector General of
Police), 169
Bhushan, Vidya, 196
Bihar Chhatra Sangharsh
Samiti (Students' Struggle
Committee), 38, 61
Bihar-wide strike, 60–61
Birla House (Gandhi Smriti),
83
Birla Mills, 7, 9, 26, 45, 149
Birla textile mills, 6
workers' group, 6–8
Bombay, 133
Brahmin, 14, 80, 117

Central Bureau of
Intelligence (CBI), 22
Central Committee of CPI
(ML), 198, 201–2
Chamars, 77, 144, 148
Chander, Ram, 48–49
Chandi, 24, 116, 118, 121–
23, 125

Chandni Chowk, 53
chaprasis, 55
childhood memories, of
Arjun, 80–96
Chinese Communist Party, 31
Churchill, Winston, 167
CIA, 26–27
class relations in rural areas,
24, 116, 119, 121
Cohn-Bendit, Daniel, 19
Communist Party of India
(CPI), 4, 69, 175, 177
Communist Party of India
(Marxist) or CPI (M), 3, 6,
41, 45, 69, 119
Communist Party of India
(Marxist–Leninist) (CPI
[ML]), 28, 50–51, 55, 120,
137–38, 148, 154, 163,
178, 183, 186, 193, 203
Congress Party, 61, 116, 119,
121, 204
Constitution Club, 22, 26
Cuban revolution, 35

Dang, Hari, 101–2, 107
Debray, Régis, 35
Delhi bandh, 61, 78, 150
Delhi bandh protest, 45, 47,
49–51
Delhi Committee, 146–47
Delhi CPI (ML), 150, 201

Delhi Development Authority (DDA), 156
Delhi Organizing Committee, 25
Delhi University, 7, 175
democracy, 20, 27, 47, 64–65, 140, 173, 179, 190–92, 200, 204–5, 208–9
Desai, Morarji, 198
Devi, Ratan, 167
dictatorship, 11, 20, 33, 75, 145, 153, 176–77, 179, 187, 190
Din, Bhagwan, 115–16, 121–22, 124, 126
Diwali, 131
Dodi Tal, 102–4
Doon School, 42, 53, 61, 68, 78, 91–92, 99–101, 108
  entertainment night, 112
  homosexuality, 108–11
  midterm treks, 102–7
  residential houses, 101
  routine of, 101
Doon School Express, 41, 97
Dussehra celebrations, 93
Dyer, Colonel Reginald, 167

Emergency law, 73
Emergency period, 73–79, 136, 160, 178
  arrests and torture, 73–74, 142, 178
  CPI (ML) and, 148–55
  demonstrations against, 76
existentialism, 20

Faiz-e-Ilahi mosque, 163, 166, 168
family-planning programme, 143–46, 151, 156
  forcible sterilizations, 144–46, 149, 151, 160–61, 182, 186, 188, 194, 195, 203
  targets, 143–44
family history, of Arjun, 81–89
Fanon, Frantz, 35
fascism, 41
Fernandes, George, 39–40, 152–55, 198, 207–9
freedom of assembly, 174
freedom of speech, 173

Gandhi, Indira (also referred to as Mrs Gandhi), 9, 26, 43, 48, 61, 73, 111, 113, 119, 140, 153, 175–79, 181, 189, 192, 196–97, 204, 207–9
  anti-business policies, 188

216 | INDEX

conviction for electoral malpractices, 142
'Garibi Hatao' – 'Eliminate Poverty' electoral campaign, 139, 160, 191
nationalization of banks, 140
war against Pakistan, 139
Gandhi, Mahatma, 51, 57, 83, 114–15, 141
Gandhi, Sanjay, 61–66, 111–13, 141, 156, 169, 177, 196–97, 204, 209
family planning, 143–45
five-point programme of action, 143–44
Ganga, 102–3
Gaulle, Charles de, 19, 32
Gauri Vrat, 132
Giáp, General Võ Nguyên, 74
Girdhar Lal Panna Lal Lace & Gota factory, 158
guerrilla warfare, 76
Guevara, Che, 35
Gujarati Brahmin family, 127–29, 135
ritualistic requirements of religion, 131–33
Gujarat Nav Nirman, 37
Gupta, Kamal, 174–75, 177

Hanuman Chalisa, 95–96

Harijan basti of Shahdara, 51, 55, 126
electricity and water supply, 52
gutter condition, 52
wedding ceremony, 55–60
Harijans (people of God), 14, 77, 114, 146
political mobilization of, 17–18
as safai karamcharis, 15
socioeconomic condition of, 15
Hatim Tai's adventures, 87
Hazrat Nizamuddin Auliya dargah, 136
hedonism, 31
Hinduism, 94
Hindu–Muslim riots, 175
Hindu religion, 8
Holdsworth, Mr (Holdie), 101
Hunter Commission, 167
Hyderabad state, 81, 83–84
Banjara Hills, 84–85
feudal structure, 90
kite fighting, 84–86
Nalgonda district of, 90–91
Rasam and Alampur mangoes of, 90

Indian Civil Service (ICS), 80
Indian railway platforms, 98

Indira Gandhi's Congress, 4
individualistic anarchists, 33, 36
individual terrorism, 24
inflation, 140
Islam, 24

Jagmohan, 169
Jallianwala Bagh massacre, 167
Jama Masjid, 157
Janata Government, 205, 209
Janata Party, 198–201, 203–4
Janvaad or 'People's Democracy', 5–6, 24, 26, 40, 147–48, 158, 160, 183
Jaonli, 107
Jats, 146
Jawaharlal Nehru University (JNU), 20, 21, 74, 138
job discrimination, 14–15
Jor Bagh, New Delhi, 135, 184
journalist, 19. *See also* Rachel.
Jyoti, 70–74, 127–38, 184–91, 193, 204

Kesavananda Bharati case, 140
Khanna, Justice H.R., 140
Krantikari Harijan Sangh (Revolutionary Harijan Association), 16, 55, 146, 162, 181, 193
Krishna's teachings to Arjuna, 93
Kumhars, 144
Kunwar sena, 120

Lakshmi Bai, Rani, 175
landlordism, 120–21, 177
left-wing ideology, 15
left-wing political group, 75
Lenin, 172, 175
Lodhi Gardens, 135, 184
Lutyens, Sir Edwin, 135

Madras Presidency, 80
Mahabharata, 93, 152
Mahamrityunjaya mantra, 94–95
Maintenance of Internal Security Act (MISA), 178
Majnu-ka-Tila (Lover's Hill), 14
Mao Tse-Tung, 31, 76, 120, 175
Martyn, Jack, 113
Marxism, 6, 15, 24, 31, 33, 74, 124, 159, 172–73
Marxism, as a revolutionary philosophy, 33
mass mobilization and mass movements, 23, 25

Mazumdar, Charu, 23, 36, 154, 202
Meins, Holger, 36
Molotov cocktail, 37, 44, 163, 208
morality or immorality of a person, 131
mountaineering expeditions, 107
Muslim neighbourhoods, 161
Muslims, 3, 86, 135, 144, 157, 161, 179, 183, 194–96
Muzaffarnagar, 182, 193–94, 196–97, 203

Nagarjuna Sagar dam, 83
Narain, Raj, 142
Narayan, Jayaprakash (JP), 37, 60–61, 73, 141, 145, 150, 188, 191, 198
    Total Revolution movement, 76, 78, 141, 175, 203
Narayanpet Samasthan, 81
nationalist movement, 81
national railway strike, 40, 150
    arrest and imprisonment, 49
    mobilizing for, 42–47
Navratri, 131–32
Naxalbari uprising, 7, 24, 119–20, 124–25, 140

Naxalite killer squads, 9
Naxalite movement, 23, 40, 52, 69
Naxalites, 36, 40, 52, 69, 120–21, 123–26, 146, 150, 190
New Delhi, 134–35. *See also* beautification of capital
Nizam of Hyderabad, 82

O'Dwyer, Sir Michael, 167–68
Officer of the British Empire (OBE), 81
Ohnesorg, Benno, 32
Oxford University, 1, 42, 78

Paris Commune of 1871, 32
pro-Russian communists, 26
Provincial Armed Constabulary (PAC), 48, 140, 195
Psycho (film), 112
purabias, 6–7, 10, 12, 45

Quit India movement, 51

Rachel, 19–22, 27–28, 29–38, 43, 172, 191, 204
Rajokri, 142, 144, 146
Ramayana, 93
Ranvir sena, 120

Rao, Raja Ramchander, 81, 90
Rashtrapati Bhavan, 1
Rashtriya Swayamsewak
   Sangh (RSS), 76, 175–76,
   180
Ray, A.N., 140
Ravana, 93–94
Red Army Faction, 35
   bombings and shootings in
      Germany, 36
   Regeneration movement, 37
Representation of the People
   Act, 142
revolutionary ideas, 2, 34
revolutionary movement, 1, 73
rheumatic fever, 129
rheumatoid arthritis, 132
rickshaw-pullers of Shahdara,
   53–54
   strike by, 53–54
Rishikesh, 103
road licence fees, 53–54
Rouge, Dany le, 32

safai karamcharis, 15–16
   strike by, 17
safe houses, 18, 75, 138, 147,
   149–52, 154, 162, 170,
   183, 201
safe huts, 75
Sahibganj, 144

Sanyal, Kanu, 23
Savarna sena, 120
Section 144 Criminal
   Procedure Code, 47
Seelampur, 15, 24, 51–52,
   55–56, 60, 75, 126, 146–
   47, 162, 180, 193, 205,
   209
Seetharamaiah, Kondapalli, 23
Sewak, Ram, 15–18, 24–25,
   41, 48–49, 52, 55, 75–77,
   114, 142, 150, 163–66,
   180–82, 193–96, 199, 205
   early childhood and family,
      116–17
   mobilization of poor for
      revolutionary change,
      125
   safai karamchari job, 118
   schooling, 118
   as sweeper in Delhi, 126
Shah Commission, 168–69
Shah of Iran, 32
sharecroppers, 115
Shivananda Ashram, 92–93
Shiva Tandava Stotram,
   93–94
Singh, Bhagat, 175
Singh, Dharam, 124
Singh, Gurdial, 101–2
Singh, Manmohan, 210

Singh, Ranbir, 121–22, 124
Singh, Thakur Dharam, 115–16, 120
Singh, Udham, 168
Sinha, Satyanarayan, 23, 149
Sisters and Brothers of the Dominican Order, 83
social discrimination, 56
social justice, 17, 206, 208–9
social worker, 136
Sorbonne Occupation Committee, 32
Speakers' Corner, London, 8
spiritual procedures to heal, 129–31
Stalin, Joseph, 191
state-sponsored violence, 49
St Stephen's College, 7, 42, 78
student movement, 19
Sultana, Rukshana, 161
Sun Tzu, 76
The Art of War, 74
Swadeshi Mills railway colony, 43–44
Swadeshi Textile Mills, 9, 22, 26, 39, 149, 170
  management and working condition, 9
  strike, 10–14, 61
  trade unions, 9

Tamta, B.R. (Commissioner of the Municipal Corporation), 169
trade unionism
  at Birla Mills, 6–9
  at Swadeshi Textile Mills, 9–10
Turkman gate demolition and rioting, 157, 161–69, 171, 174, 183, 192, 196

unemployment, 140
Uttarkashi, 103

Vajpayee, Atal Bihari, 199–201, 203
Vietnam War, 32
Vrindavan, 77–79

Wazirpur factories, 45
Women's liberation, 20
workers' and peasants' movement, 4, 8
workers' militancy, 10–13

Yadav, Brijendra, 195
young 'revolutionaries', 7
Youth Congress, 61, 65

Zakir Husain College, 3, 157–58, 162

About the Author

ASHOK CHAKRAVARTI is an economist who has been providing policy advice to countries, mainly in the African region, for the past forty years. He is the author of books published in the UK and USA, which focus on the central role of institutions in economic development. He is currently senior economic advisor to the Government of Zimbabwe, based in Harare.